Praise for **Breakaway**

Breakaway is a revolutionary book. By focusing on the role of speed and expertise in delivering value to customers fast, Fred has turned the conventional wisdom of business change completely on its head...a visionary, practical, and exciting tool that will transform business learning and development forever.

A. Reed Hayes
President and Chief Operating Officer,
National Restaurant Association Education Foundation

As one of the founders of Precision Response Corporation, a leader in outsourced integrated customer care for over 18 years, I have seen, first-hand, the importance of people in the customer equation, and encourage business leaders to follow Fred's secrets for success.

David Epstein
Chief Executive Officer,
Precision Response Corporation

Breakaway

*Using Speed and Expertise to
Deliver Value to Customers—Fast*

Charles L. Fred

Grand River Publishing, LLC
Boulder, Colorado

Library of Congress Cataloging-in-Publication Data is on
file with the publisher.

ISBN 0-929290-06-2

Printed in the United States of America.

To Julie, my eternal friend, mentor, and partner,
your support and love made this possible

Contents

Breakaway

Chapter 7
The Leadership Agenda: Taking People from Where They Are To Where They Need to Be—Fast

"Things may come to those

who wait, but only the things

left by those who hustle."

Abraham Lincoln

Acknowledgments

The journey to create this book began on January 7, 1993. Julie, my wife and master motivator, left the book *Publish and Flourish* by Garry Schaeffer and Tony Alessandra on my desk, with an encouraging note written on the inside flap. From that moment forward, this book has been under construction. The fact that the book now exists, after seven years of development and research, is truly a result of the people who supported and pushed me forward.

My three wonderful children have encouraged me with smiles through office doors, scribbled many notes of encouragement, and have graciously given up precious time that could otherwise have been spent together. I owe them so much for their understanding.

Robert Davis, the chief architect of the final version of this book, has been brilliant in his ability to craft a plan I could work with. His coaching and encouragement facilitated the completion of this work. Without his guidance, it would still be a tangled manuscript.

James Keener, my friend and publisher, has been with me on this project from the beginning. His early leadership and expertise enabled the research and disparate ideas to take the shape of a manuscript.

Breakaway

I am grateful for Barbara Ellington and her tireless efforts poring over the original manuscript. Her editorial guidance and creative ideas established an innovative direction for the book and the overall message.

The initial research and the notion of a proficiency threshold can be credited to Dr. Stephen Kirkpatrick. His background and genius regarding learning segmentation and the link between learning and performance helped shape many of the ideas in this text.

I would like to acknowledge Dan Guenther and his passion to help me advance as a writer. His past literary success and his encouragement filled my mental fuel tank more than once.

The associates of International Learning Systems and specifically, Peggy Steele, taught me about the corporate education business. The introductions to many of the references in this book are a result of my experiences with this team, and I thank them for sharing their time and their knowledge.

My time with the people of Omega Performance has not only reshaped this book, but my understanding of educational excellence. I thank the members of this world-class team for taking me under their wing, teaching me about the financial services industry, and preparing me for the next leg of my journey. Specifically, I thank David Bennett for believing that I could lead the company he co-founded twenty-five years ago and for his untiring support of this book.

I also want to recognize the incredibly talented team that produced the final package. Michele Wetherbee created the striking book cover and excited the team to think differently regarding a new look and feel. Patricia Heinicke's editorial skills greatly advanced the message, and Debbie Remmen brought the graphics and layout of the book to a truly professional level.

Foreword

Mr. Fred offers readers something invaluable: insight into how to gain a formidable competitive advantage based on a new understanding of human performance. There is widespread agreement that the new economy is transforming the nature of business, and that technology will play an increasingly important role in that transformation. The author contends that while technology is critical, it is not nearly as important as speed and expertise. This book focuses on the intersection of these two elements.

Although this book highlights companies that have "broken from the pack" in a number of industries, its findings are especially important for companies providing financial services. In the next five years the market changes these organizations will face will dwarf those of the previous five years. For many these changes will seem an incomprehensible tangle of convergence, consolidation, and technology. Without dismissing these complexities, the truth is that they are trumped by something relatively simple to understand, yet difficult to deliver on: *execution*.

In 1998 the Council on Financial Competition published its landmark study *The Center of the Dashboard: Aligning Sales, Service and Brand to Combat Customer Attrition*. It examined the changing nature of customer loyalty in what it called a "frictionless economy," where consumer choices in financial services are rapidly increasing while the costs to consumers of switching providers are rapidly decreasing. The study found that retaining existing customers accounted for more than 75 percent of shareholder value, whereas activities aimed at acquiring new customers and reducing costs accounted for only 11 percent and 6 percent of shareholder value respectively.

The study found that "most organizations wildly overstate the loss of customer activity that is truly uncontrollable." In fact less than 5 percent of defection is truly beyond an institution's control. Financial institutions have for years been guilty of underestimating the value of retaining existing customers and overestimating the value of acquiring new customers. Many organizations do not appreciate that selling new products to new customers can be up to twice as expensive as the sale of that same product to an existing customer. They instinctively think that the grass is "greener on the other side," when in fact the vast majority of opportunity lies on their side of the fence within their existing customer base. With product barriers falling, even customers with an "average" demographic profile can be quite profitable if an organization understands the changing financial status of these customers and develops market and product strategies to meet these changing needs.

The implications of these findings are profound, for they highlight the importance of employee execution in the delivery of financial services in two critical areas: first, in flawlessly performing service recovery actions that are "hardwired" into employee disciplines, and second, in proactively managing customer relationships to maximize their value over time.

The foundation of customer retention is the ability of employees to act decisively and appropriately when things go wrong. Customers rarely switch providers when a problem is solved in a timely and satisfactory manner—service recovery paradoxically can *increase* customer loyalty dramatically. In other words, the ability of financial services employees to execute properly in the moment of crisis is critical to shareholder value. The vast majority of customers will give you the opportunity to set things right, and indeed may have a greater appreciation for the organization because the problem has been corrected in a satisfactory manner. However, failure to execute in that moment of truth will destroy customer loyalty. There is a good deal of evidence to suggest that many unsatisfied customers will eagerly share their unsatisfactory experience with others, with a potential negative snowballing effect on brand image and institutional reputation.

It is tempting and specious to think of customer retention primarily as a service quality issue. True competitive advantage is to be found through proactive sales disciplines by early "onboarding" of customers to ensure they have been sold the right products, that is, those that truly satisfy their needs. Customer-focused institutions will further strengthen their relationship with customers by using "triggers" to identify when a customer's life needs are changing, with appropriate product solutions ready to respond to these changing needs. Once again, though technology is critical to these disciplines, at the heart of customer retention is employee *execution* at key moments in the customer relationship.

Many organizations have attempted to build their brand without really taking employee execution into account. "Most institutions wrongly focus on advertising to migrate their brands," the Council on Financial Competition notes. "Market leaders recognize that consistency between internal processes and external promises is central to successful branding." The truth is that customers have much greater interaction with financial institutions through the branches and call centers, and through regular communication such as account statements, than they do through interacting with an organization's advertising and marketing departments. "In financial services (and other service businesses), building brand is a matter of execution, not mere communication," the Council notes. Put differently, employee execution is at the heart of shareholder value.

This book offers a blueprint for gaining significant competitive advantage through exemplary execution—what the author calls *breakaway performance*. The key to competing at the intersection of speed and expertise is in understanding that the systems companies have used for more than fifty years to prepare their employees to deliver in the marketplace are grossly inadequate for the rigors of the new economy, especially in an industry like financial services that is being transformed every day. These old paradigms are based on learning theory that is completely divorced from actual on-the-job performance, not to mention bottom-line sales results. The author introduces a new set of learning disciplines and measures rooted in providing value to customers faster than the competition.

The premise of the book is elegantly simple—those institutions that learn how to train employees quickly and efficiently as the market continually changes around them will have a distinct competitive advantage. Put another way, if your institution takes six months to arm your employees with the tools to be skilled in selling a new product set and your competitor can get their employees to the same skill level in three months, your competitor will enjoy significant competitive advantage. Companies no longer have the luxury of comprehensive training programs. The pace of product and service change simply demands a paradigm shift in the ability of institutions to get their people fully competent. Speed to proficiency is the critical success variable. Those institutions that figure out how to deliver at the high end of the speed/competency matrix will be the winners.

Omega's mantra for twenty-five years has been one of improving the performance of people through efficient and accelerated learning methodologies. We understand the need to bring employees to an optimum level of expertise in the features and benefits of a product set, for example, while being highly cognizant of the time/cost equation. The same metrics apply to training in the soft skills that underlie all selling. In other words, "How much do they need to know to optimize their performance?" This book articulates that challenge clearly, and provides the reader with insights into how to manage the balance.

David G. Falwell
President and Chief Executive Officer
Omega Performance Corporation

How to Use This Book

This book is designed for the business reader, to be read in the time it takes to fly from Chicago to San Francisco or Denver to Miami. Its purpose is to excite a new set of beliefs regarding the education of today's worker and to catalyze the change that is necessary to compete in today's economy. As you read, seek the nuggets that will accelerate your current performance and learning efforts. I look forward to hearing from you in our specially designed communication space at breakawayperformance.com. This site is designed to help the reader accumulate experience with the concepts in this text. You can link to key thought leaders, find soul mates, and articulate your experience or frustration with the current situation at your enterprise.

Get fast, and break away!

Charles L. Fred

Introduction

Humans, with the knowledge and

skills that enable them to deliver

on the promises made to

customers, are without a doubt

the primary source of value in

business today.

The new economy is driven by the connection of speed and expertise. Humans, with the knowledge and skills that enable them to deliver on the promises made to customers, are without a doubt the primary source of economic value in business today. In a labor market that rewards the free agent, with unemployment low and technological change accelerating beyond our wildest imagination, a proficient worker—armed with the tools to learn as fast as the economy changes—becomes the catalytic ingredient for a business to grow.

Today start-ups thirst for the critical skills to build a business, knowing that if they lack proficient workers to enter the marketplace and immediately gain customer attention, they are dead. Blue chips attempt the daunting task of preparing a work force to support the new digital world, while keeping the old processes alive for the thousands of customers who still need them. Nearly everything we thought we knew about the economy ten years ago is now open to question. But one thing is clear: the basic ability of an enterprise to survive and grow is a function of its know-how—that is, how quickly it can get its people to learn something new and transfer this knowledge to its customers. In our rapidly changing marketplace, it is deadly to be comfortable with yesterday's pace for learning.

This book offers a new set of rules based on new insights about work and learning. I start with the view that most training and development efforts in the business world are woefully insufficient to handle the speed of today's economy. A fundamental shift away from event-based training must occur. Competitive companies must begin to focus on a learner's ability to accumulate experience *rapidly*. They must be able to manage the learning process, which begins with the introduction of new information, services, and products, and continues until a learner can actually deliver value to customers. This fundamental change in focus will push a company toward the integration of work and learning, where the two efforts become virtually seamless. The amount of time it takes a single learner to progress through this process will determine the capacity of the company as a whole to learn faster.

Put your skepticism on hold and ask yourself if you and the people of your company can reach proficiency at the speed of the new economy. Can your current system for developing people fulfill the growth requirements of your shareholders, satisfy anxious customers, and excite your workers enough to keep them? If not, I offer new ideas to help improve the pace of performance, the speed by which you can change, and the overall competitiveness of your firm.

The Intersection of Speed and Expertise

Speed is now equal to quality

in its value to consumers

and—for the delivery of a

service—consistently

outweighs price.

The mile run is a grueling track and field race. I had the good fortune to compete in this event during my college days. Since then I've used it as a metaphor to articulate the advantage created by delivering value to customers significantly faster than your competition.

Halfway through the notorious four-lap race, at the beginning of the third lap, a phenomenon called the *breakaway* occurs. Up to this point nearly all runners are still tightly packed together, jockeying for position, cruising at a pace that pushes each runner's pulse between 160 and 190 beats per minute. Lactic acid is accumulating in the large leg muscles, lungs burn as they are filled to capacity and emptied every second, and each runner's brain constantly takes stock of the body's condition even as it craves oxygen itself. At this point, every runner in the pack must make a very tough decision: to summon a burst of speed and attempt to win by *breaking away* from the other runners, or to let others go ahead and rationalize that winning is not really so important.

The breakaway is more than a *physical* action; it is the most significant *mental* challenge a runner faces. All the bodily pain and mental anguish must be put aside if one is to break away and win. The breakaway lasts only 20 to 30 seconds, but it is devastating for those who choose to avoid it, and inspiring for those who choose to go faster and become part of the lead pack. The leaders move continuously ahead of those left behind, drawing strength from the exhilarating sensation of actually being in a position to win. Their attention is focused outward, toward the future, on reaching the finish line first. Those who follow quickly become consumed with physical exhaustion and the deep disappointment of watching all opportunity for victory vanish. Their attention is focused inward, toward the past, on wondering why they didn't have the strength to stay with the leaders.

A similar phenomenon occurs in the marketplace. Many companies compete in a relatively equal position of market share and growth, with comparable equipment, technological sophistication, and office layouts. Suddenly, one company makes a significant move in as little as two quarters, and few competitors can keep up. Just like the runner who initiates the breakaway, a company that quickly sets itself apart from its competitors becomes *outwardly* focused on winning. People in these organizations typically have higher morale, are more customer oriented, and understand how their daily contribution fits into the overall competitive plan. Conversely, organizations that have fallen behind tend to focus on all the *internal* issues that put them in a losing position. They typically engage in cost-reduction measures and reorganization aimed at eliminating those perceived to be responsible for the deteriorating performance. These are the companies that will continually seek the quick fix.

What enables one company to break away from the rest? I contend that it is increasingly the *ability of people to deliver more value to customers in a shorter period of time*. As the core of our economy continues its shift from the production of goods to the delivery of services, the experience, creativity, and adaptability of the performing human is rapidly becoming the most valuable business asset. Services don't exist until they are performed, and customers judge the service by the performance. Production, delivery, and consumption are often concurrent actions. Therefore, attracting, acquiring, and retaining customers depends on the expertise of the person performing the service. If the time it takes you to deliver a product or service is longer than your competitors', or if your workers are less than proficient, you will lose the race. You will watch from the back of the pack as your competition pulls farther and farther ahead.

A breakaway is initiated by building the basic capacity of an organization and its people to get their jobs done much more quickly and effectively—to deliver greater value to customers faster than the competition. Organizations in the lead set the pace because they have created the wherewithal to recruit, develop, and sustain a premier work force. The followers can only focus on the daunting challenge of staying in the race and attempting to keep their workers from defecting to the leader's camp. Building a proficient workforce fast therefore stimulates a number of advantages that, once created, are extraordinarily difficult for the competition to duplicate.

The Need for Speed

Fred Smith, the founder of Federal Express, changed more than the way a package is delivered. He, and others who followed, fundamentally changed the expectations of consumers. No longer are quality and price the only drivers of competition. Speed has now become a primary variable in consumers' perception of value. Consumers expect and demand smart employees to handle their requests immediately—with one call to the toll-free service line, instant availability of inventory, and immediate and accurate information. Speed of service, product availability, and information are becoming critical factors in a company's

The most important—and
vulnerable—connection
between strategy and
execution is the actual
performance of people.

ability to compete. Pick any service offered today and consider how your expectations of availability and delivery have changed. These expectations are continuously reinforced as consumers reward providers that offer services faster than the competition. Speed is now equal to quality in its value to consumers and—for the delivery of a service—consistently outweighs price. The source of the demand for speed is consumers, and their definition of value consistently includes time—their time.

This change in our perception of time has been accelerated by information readily available at the click of a mouse or a touch of a button. For example, until recently, the average time to apply for and receive approval for a standard home mortgage was five working days. Nearly every banking institution operated at this pace, and banks did not agonize about offering faster loan approval as a part of their value proposition. Instead, their focus was on accurate service, product differentiation, and rate offerings. Today, however, loan approvals are nearly instantaneous, and the consumer's expectations regarding the speed of all of the follow-on services necessary to complete a loan transaction continue to escalate. Technology has fundamentally altered consumers' perception of what constitutes value in financial services.

The need to deliver value to customers faster has moved well past the consumer model and now permeates every enterprise whose customers value their time. Business-to-business product and service companies are now under great pressure to deliver value rapidly. Wholesale utility providers, Internet infrastructure manufacturers, and even the big consulting firms are grappling with the consequences of their lack of speed. Their destiny, like that of the fast-moving consumer service businesses, is now inextricably tied to how quickly they can retool to meet the speed demands of the enterprise customer.

Well over a decade ago, firms began to grasp the advantage of bringing products to market faster than the competition. Companies that have adopted speed to market as an operating principle have found that it catalyzes growth in their profits and loyalty in their workers. Today, leaders are beginning to understand that advantage lies not just in the faster development of new products and services, but also in the faster development in the expertise of the people who deliver those products and services. Great improvements have been made in the science and process of developing new products, but the real opportunity to outperform the competition comes from the up-to-date know-how of the worker who serves the customer. Customers not only want services fast, they want these services delivered by competent people. The advantages of placing a product or service in the hands of a customer before the competition does are so glaringly clear that one would assume that ensuring worker proficiency in the delivery process would be a high business priority. More often than not, however, the proficiency of the workers who deliver or support the new offering does not satisfy the customer.

One company that performs with the expertise of its people is the Home Depot. Today it is the largest home improvement retailer in North America, operating nearly 900 warehouse-style stores across the country. For six consecutive years, Home Depot has been ranked by *Fortune* magazine as "America's Most Admired Specialty Retailer."[1] For me, the proof of their success is in the value

I receive from their employees. I can sketch my latest home improvement idea on a napkin, bring it to their employees, and they will help me bring it to life. The knowledge and proficiency of these retail workers are clearly why so many people pack their stores each week. Service is delivered through the proficiency of each store employee. Other mega-retailers offer the same products, have the same gigantic warehouses, and in many cases reside in the same general location. But Home Depot's success, its place at the head of the pack, drives them to continually push the pace. Not only do they arguably have the best-prepared workforce, but they have now expanded the value of this expertise by offering education to customers. In July 1999, the Home Depot began to offer free, in-depth, hands-on home improvement classes to customers, taught by their own proficient and capable people.

Expertise may therefore become the most recognizable element of a company's brand. The best enhancement and extension of a brand in a knowledge-based economy is not the look and feel of marketing collateral and products, but instead the reputation and knowledge of the people selling and servicing those products. Proficient employees leave a long and lasting impression on customers. This impression, coupled with a strong brand, can build loyalty and retention levels that are impossible for the competition to match.

Companies that can tout the know-how of their work force, not just the features and benefits of their products or services, are realizing great dividends in the marketplace. And organizations that truly have proficient workers are becoming market leaders. New Century Energies, the large gas and electric utility in Colorado and Texas, for example,

Speed to proficiency is more
than a theoretical advantage;
it is the most devastating
competitive weapon in a
world where the competitive
forces of scale, automation,
and capital are subordinate
to the power of a proficient
work force.

has positioned its newly formed brand as a service of smart employees. Wayne Brunetti, its creative CEO, is building his company not only as a utility for the future but as a brand known for highly competent people who can safely and efficiently provide service to the public.[2] This is a keen strategy for overcoming a very formidable barrier of public skepticism, as the wary public critically eyes new, unstable competitors in the utility industry.

Marketing human know-how is only a competitive advantage if a system is in place to actually create proficient workers. Marketers can only fool the wise consumer once. A company with a reputation for uninformed or disenfranchised workers will have a very tough time reversing the negative perception already created.

A Crash at the Intersection

It is obvious that a new system for rapidly developing the workforce is needed, and yet many business leaders are preoccupied with activities that seem much more important, at least in the short term. They overlook the fact that the most important—and vulnerable—connection between strategy and execution is the actual performance of people. Senior managers have consistently failed to consider the capacity of their people to learn faster.[3] The intersection between work and learning, between an individual's job and the promise of swift service to the consumer, poses a significant challenge to the leaders of today's organizations. In this economy the importance of a skilled, proficient work force, capable of decision making, problem solving, and self-direction in handling the primary tasks of their jobs, will continually escalate. Most of the traditional methods to develop these capabilities in an organization work too slowly. Staying competitive demands that people learn faster than is possible with traditional learning models. Keeping the speed requirement from crashing into the training department will require leaders to refocus on the basic performance capacity of the organization and to seek creative ways to help workers match their learning process with the speed of change.

The economy of speed offers a new and incremental advantage. Any organization that can quickly develop a critical mass of proficient workers will always be in the lead pack and in a position to dominate the marketplace. Proficient workers speed things up: organizational change, operational improvement, problem solving, and delivery of service all happen faster. When you shorten the time it takes for workers to become proficient, the capital and resources required to introduce a new product, maintain operations and infrastructure, and perform a service are also proportionally reduced. "Speed to proficiency" is more than a theoretical advantage; it is the most devastating competitive weapon in a world where the competitive forces of scale, automation, and capital are subordinate to the power of a proficient work force.

2

New Rules
for a New World

Survival for any company

today hinges on the

connection between the

promises made to customers

and the ability of the work

force to deliver on that

promise.

One day when I was a senior manager at the telecommunications firm US West, I was sifting through my office mail when I noticed a handwritten note among the stack of laser-printed documents. The note, sent from a front-line network technician named Kyle, was written on the back of a blank work order.

> Dear Mr. Fred,
>
> I recently attended the training class you've sponsored on Team Problem Solving. I know your intentions are good, but I wanted to give you some feedback.
>
> I work ten hours a day out of my truck. Nearly everything I need to complete a work order fits someplace in this rig. The instructor said to keep the class materials handy over the next few weeks for reference. Where do I put this three-ring binder? To be honest with you, I highly doubt that I will ever refer to these materials. Would you like them back for the next class to use?
>
> I think your vision of us needing problem solving and productivity skills is OK, but did you really think this class would make us better at bringing service to our customers?
>
> Our biggest problem or skill shortage is knowing how to install these new remote terminals. It takes twice as long to turn them up [install them] as the old ones. We keep telling customers that we will get them telephone service faster but the only training we get is this problem solving crap. Every day I have to face the homeowner that is waiting for phone service. If you want to help, get us the training we need to get these people hooked up faster!
>
> Thanks for listening. I just thought you should know that we don't think much of this kind of training.
>
> Kyle

Breakaway

When Kyle sent me this note, the Colorado Public
Utilities Commission was investigating US West's poor
performance on "held orders"—accounts for which we
could not deliver basic telephone service to customers in
thirty days or less. The network technicians were under
extreme pressure to correct an embarrassing problem and
were routinely working overtime. Compounding this situ-
ation was a fourteen-state promotion of US West's new
service-quality initiative that promised customers dramatic improvements in service.

Seven months before receiving Kyle's letter, I had
decided to embark on a site-wide training program to
help workers solve problems more quickly and effectively,
in part because our annual employee survey had indicat-
ed a general lack of problem-solving skills among the
work force. It seemed obvious that our employees needed
problem-solving training. Kyle's note, however, made
what seemed obvious look outright ridiculous. General
problem-solving skills may have helped some employee
sometime in the future, but workers right now lacked the
specific skills to deliver what the company was promising
to the customer today.

Moreover, after looking into how much training our
network technicians received for technical service skills, I
had discovered that little or none was being provided—
indeed, almost all of our training budget was set aside for
management development, rather than training the front
line. Considering how little training the technicians were
receiving, the fact that most of it wasn't linked to providing value to the customer was appalling. Yet prior to
Kyle's missive, I considered the problem-solving course to

be an enlightened management action that was directly aligned with our organization's belief in lifelong learning, a universal subsidy to the overall company. Had the promise to customers been the driving force behind my decision for training in problem solving, Kyle would have been receiving technical training on the new equipment with elements of problem solving built in. The primary purpose of his learning would have been to get service to customers faster, a direct advantage for the company.

Linking Development to Delivery of Value

Stiff competition presents a challenge to many businesses. In most markets, customers have many options from which to choose. Any gap between what has been promised and what is delivered will provoke customers to switch. This kind of defection occurs on every level—from an individual finding a new Internet provider to a large corporation switching travel agencies. Survival for any company today hinges on the connection between the promises made to customers and the ability of the work force to deliver on that promise.

Great strides have been made in the past decade in understanding and defining the "value chain," the collective process within an enterprise that creates value for a customer. The notion of a "value proposition," the ultimate promise made to customers, has also become common marketing language in most organizations. Few organizations, however, have recognized the development of their people as a key link in the value chain.

The training of the work

force is usually viewed as a

necessary chore or

sometimes as an enlightened

perk, rather than a

strategically critical link in

the value chain.

More precisely, training is rarely positioned as the primary means to deliver on the promises made to customers. The training of the work force is usually viewed as a necessary chore or sometimes as an enlightened perk, rather than a strategically critical link in the value chain. Although marketing, product development, branding, and promotion are all considered vital priorities for revenue growth, the ability of the work force to deliver is almost always a secondary consideration. Typical training events are therefore designed in reaction to a marketing campaign or a new service introduction already underway. From the outset, the learning event is disconnected from the original promise to the customer—witness my problem-solving class at US West. The reactionary design and development of training has become an operational habit—a habit that for most of us seems perfectly normal.

Earlier in this century, unsystematic on-the-job training was replaced with professionally designed training "events," which now make up the bulk of U.S. corporate training.[1] In our current frame of thinking, little training occurs outside the defined boundaries of a learning event. Because we have chosen to see workers and their learning as something finite and constant, event-based training has been a perfect solution. Think about the sequential method of the traditional employee training session. A training need appears, a course is developed, and over a period of time employees are trained. Some will take the course many months before they need to apply the skills, while others wait until well after the training is needed. The number of students per session is dictated by the availability of both learners and teacher.

But today, most business operations cannot operate in this kind of "batch" mode. They need to place proficient workers when and where the need exists. In today's environment, few people have time for extracurricular events of any kind, let alone training. Much has changed from the days when you could "schedule" people into training and provide someone to back them up on the job. Faced with the competition, few managers can afford to take employees away from customers or the front line. Business leaders are aware that it takes too long to train workers in the traditional method, but most are using an old set of rules to fix the problem.

"Training takes too long!" This is the characteristic response of frustrated decision-makers to current training solutions, which are simply too slow for the breakneck pace of business today. Yet all too often the solution is short-sighted: simply shorten the time it takes to get people trained. This reactive solution assumes that learning can occur instantaneously, in a one-time event. To accommodate the need for an increased pace, classes that were once designed for five consecutive days of delivery have now been condensed to two days, maybe three. Each time a "quick fix" is applied and a course is shortened, there is an illusion that learning has occurred, and in less time. Statements like, "We are training our people faster" corroborate this false assumption.

Beyond this compression of class time, there are usually no other innovations in course content or design. The result is like drinking from a fire hose: the rush of data is overwhelming, and not enough information is retained to apply back on the job. The condensed version of the course wastes not only two days of valuable learning time but also two days of service or production. When people return to the job, expected efficiencies do not materialize because little, if any, learning actually occurred during the compressed course. Strangely, this failure often goes undetected because results are rarely measured back on the job.

The implications of this are staggering. Imagine a service company receiving an order for a particular service through its in-bound call center. The order fulfillment process records the order and places it in a delivery queue but then abandons any follow-up on the performance or delivery of the service—there are never any checks to see if the actual service was completed and acceptable to the customer. This company's chances of survival are slim. But this is precisely the circumstance in which businesses and organizations delivering traditional training events find themselves. Giving employee training its proper place in the value chain requires more than speed; it requires an understanding of how people learn most effectively.

The Accumulation of Experience

Even though few managers truly believe in instant proficiency, their attitudes toward training often seem to contradict their innate common sense. They target nearly all their training effort and investment on the initial act of training, and as a result, much of the roughly $60 billion spent each year on training is lost because most of what is presented in this initial act is not thoroughly learned, and

Learning is not fundamentally integrated with strategic business needs, and so the employee's educational experiences never reach the critical mass required for the training to be effective.

what is learned is not retained.[2] If decision makers knew that nearly 80 percent of their investment is lost within forty-eight hours after each class, they would take this problem more seriously. With little or no reinforcement of the training material, retention falls at an accelerating rate. G. V. Goddard calls this rate the Forgetting Curve.[3] Figure 2.1 shows the rapid loss of retention, and the risks for retaining so little that proficiency is never attained.

The Forgetting Curve

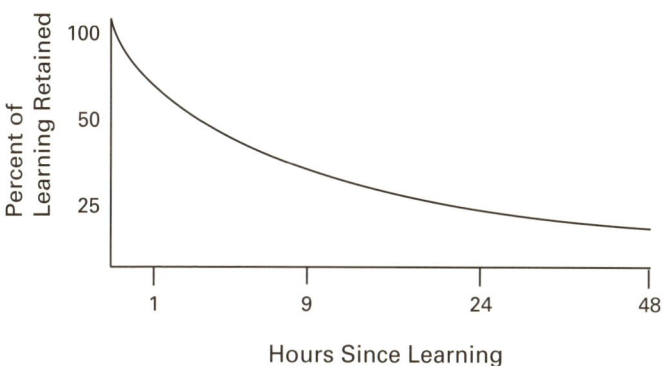

Hours Since Learning

Figure 2.1

The problem is that learners forget what they have learned before it can be integrated into their jobs. In traditional training, this problem is often described by saying that classroom learning needs to be "reinforced" on the job or it will be lost. The implication is that the job should change to support learning. In fact, it is the learning that needs to change to support the job. The problem isn't simply lack of reinforcement. The problem is that learning is not fundamentally integrated with strategic business needs, and so the employee's educational experiences never reach the critical mass required for the training to be effective. For learning to "stick," for knowledge to really be retained, the learner needs a series of learning experiences in close proximity. In other words, knowledge is a waste if it is not converted into performance.

What's missing from our current learning systems? I'll go into more detail later, but let's go through the highlights now. Adults move through four phases as they learn. In the first phase, new information is *introduced* to our cognitive processes. This may be information about a new product or new service, or a new theory. We progress into the second phase, called *assimilation*, in which the human memory combines the new information with previous experiences and learning. In phase three, we *translate* the new information and our previous knowledge into a job function or a particular application.

At this point, most of us can understand how the new information relates to our job and what needs to be done to actually perform, but we still can't perform. Therefore, the fourth and most crucial phase is the *accumulation of experience* with the new information. Converting knowledge into performance requires experience. Across the world, the lion's share of training dollars are tied up in the first three phases, leaving the accumulation of experience mostly to chance. Yet this fourth phase will dictate whether an employee can actually deliver on the promises made to a customer.

The accumulation of experience, often completely ignored by instructional designers, is the most important step toward ensuring proficiency. Without it, a decision maker can bank on the fact that nearly all of the investment will end up wasted, and that significant additional time and money will be needed as employees grapple in the workplace to find the reinforcement and the practice that were absent in the initial training.

Focusing on Speed

When the goal of training is to develop skills *fast*— whether it be to serve the customer, improve the quality of products, or support others in the business—then priorities for learning and skill development become merged with strategic business decisions. Managers therefore approach the problem as they would any other operational constraint and apply resources directly to the workers who need it most. In contrast, when the primary purpose is to benevolently train great numbers of people in a particular course, then strategic decisions became training decisions and the operational purpose is lost in the complex process of moving a mass of people through an event.

The great news about the changes in our world and our economy is that they play right into the strengths of humans. Constant advances in technology will automate many repetitive activities required in the manufacturing and service sectors and will facilitate the movement of information, enabling people to innovate, create, and serve, all of which will become the growth and value drivers of our future.

But these advances will also require the delivery of that value *fast*. In order to achieve the rapid delivery of value

When the goal of training is

to develop skills *fast* then

priorities for learning and

skill development become

merged with strategic

business decisions.

to customers, an absolutely clear picture of the "value proposition" must be created—and all performance must be connected to it. What specific promise is the enterprise making to customers? Even innovative, highly motivated people will never create a breakaway advantage if they do not have a solid understanding of what they are supposed to deliver and why. Conversely, even tired, modestly creative workers who understand the promise can move in front of the competition.

The New Rules

If you were to pause and think seriously about the three or four things that can bring people in an organization to proficiency faster than anything else, what would they be? Over the past six years, I have asked this question of business leaders across the globe. In answering the question, none of them cited needs analysis research or a specific instructional design model, and only a handful suggested a training course. Instead, they were passionate about getting employees into practice sessions quickly, using new technology to bring information to the worker and breaking new information into sound bites while linking it with daily work activities. Most of these leaders were also excited about creating an environment where they could see the speed of their progress manifest in people who dazzle customers and exceed organizational expectations. Unfortunately, most of these discussions ended with an admission that the current training system in their organization is nothing even close to what they described as "fast."

The following rules define a new model that will help advance the learning efforts of these leaders toward fulfilling their passion for speed. The model has been pounded into shape by a number of colleagues who have worked through the nuances of the original theory and put the rules into practice. This model has enabled organizations to bring people to proficiency up to 80 percent faster than the traditional methods. As I discuss in Chapter 6, however, no single recipe or step-by-step process will drive speed to proficiency; speed will also depend on a number of additional issues relating to leadership and enthusiasm. Therefore, this model does not propose a formula, but rather it helps establish a new orientation centered on using speed and expertise to deliver value to customers, *fast*. The next three chapters of this book illuminate the following rules.

Rule 1: Establish the Proficiency Threshold

To be able to deliver value to customers, leaders must clearly understand that growth in the new economy will demand a different way of looking at the human contribution. Today's leader must clearly understand that the worker is no longer a commodity, as technology takes over that role. A leader's real job, then, is to create a team of performers who can deliver value to customers fast, and the workers' real job is to know when they have achieved the proficiency to really deliver on what has been promised.

Breakaway

A New Model
for Human Performance

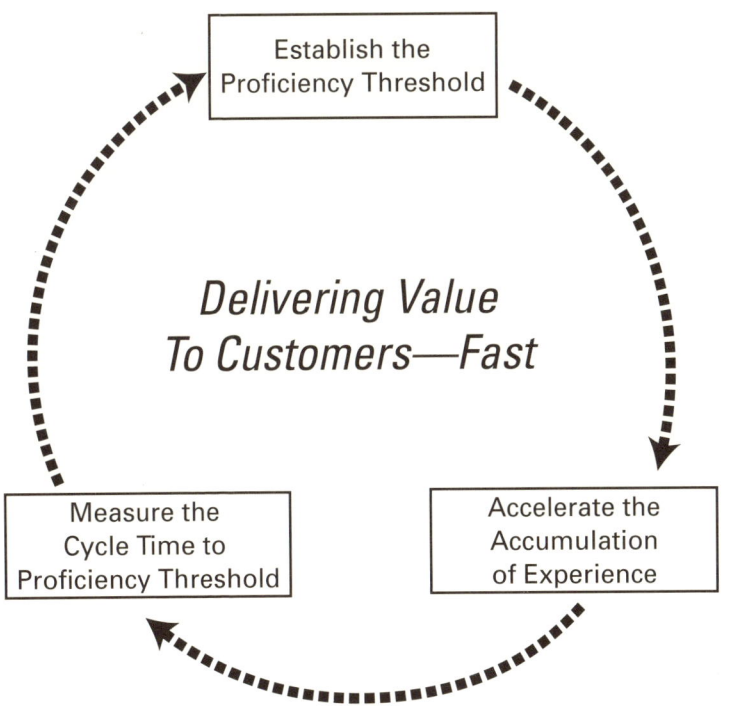

Establish the
Proficiency Threshold

*Delivering Value
To Customers—Fast*

Accelerate the
Accumulation
of Experience

Measure the
Cycle Time to
Proficiency Threshold

Figure 2.2

If you were to pause and think seriously about the three or four things that can bring people in an organization to proficiency faster than anything else, what would they be?

The point at which a person can deliver the promised value is called the *proficiency threshold*, and for the remainder of this book, I will refer to threshold proficiency as a critical point in a company's ability to compete. This milestone must be defined and understood before any precious time is spent on learning activities. The time a worker spends in any form of learning must be tied *directly* to the promises made to customers. When the connection between the training and the promises is tight, the learners immediately understand their role in delivering value to the customer, and the objective of learning and performing is literally defined by what the organization is attempting to do for its customer.

Once the overarching value proposition becomes the focus of training, the development of people to deliver on the promise becomes significantly less complex. In today's environment, all professional development activities must advance the delivery of the proposition. Any activities that are not clearly tied to the proposition should be questioned. It becomes a simple litmus test: will this help us deliver on the promise or not?

Rule 2: Accelerate the Accumulation of Experience

Accumulating enough experience to deliver on the value proposition takes a performer directly to the heart of what matters most in business learning. They can test concepts, alter approaches, fail quickly and recover quickly, and ultimately gain the needed experience to perform. Nothing about this method, however, should be left to chance. When done correctly, this phase is as strictly designed as the classroom. Imagine working and accumulating experience in an environment where your performance coach sits in the adjacent cubicle or is immediately available online. Short, reinforcing modules and reference materials are readily available on your browser, one phone call will net an immediate answer to a question, and a manager checks in to assess your progress. Focusing on the accumulation of experience is a critical shift from traditional training and is absolutely necessary to achieving breakaway performance. This reformation makes possible the true advantage for an enterprise in today's competitive environment—a reduction in the time it takes to deliver on the promises made to the market-place and to analysts, shareowners, and employees.

Rule 3: Measure Cycle Time to Proficiency Threshold

Cycle time to threshold proficiency is a metric that will drive new competitive behaviors. The metric helps rede-fine the development of people in the context of the deliv-ery of value and of time—in this case, the time it takes for individuals to prepare themselves to perform. In essence, if everyone is connected to the value proposition, then they also must deliver on the promise fast, before someone else does. This metric alone will have a profound effect on the way an organization measures its ability to compete

New Rules or Old?

Remember the good old days? The Alfred P. Sloan museum in Flint, Michigan, is a fantastic reminder of the great busi-ness days of the past. The automotive artifacts are a testa-ment of the economic opulence created by the automotive industry. From the 1930s to the 1970s, General Motors was the model for how great businesses were run, and Alfred P.

Sloan was arguably the most powerful businessman on earth. During this time, GM defined the game of business and its rules. Its success came from an economy of scale, owning the supply chain, and lifetime employment.

Today, Bill Gates and Michael Dell define the game and the rules. Within a very short time, they too may have a museum like Mr. Sloan's. The game of business is changing very rapidly. It took over forty years for a new order to overtake the business model inherited from GM. Some argue that Microsoft has already lost its dominance as the ideal model. If past economic changes are any indication of the future, those who seek to play the new game by the new rules will at the very least be in a position to recover when the contest changes again. The new rules will test some deep-seated beliefs about adult training and learning. I challenge those of you who are responsible for the competitiveness of your organization to reorient your thinking toward a new way of developing people, to build and develop a workforce that can anticipate and adapt as quickly as the economy changes.

3

Establish the
Proficiency Threshold

What promises are made to your customers?

What role do your people play in delivering on that promise?

Which of your competitors makes a similar promise?

What happens if your competition delivers on that promise first?

Recently I was searching for a portable projector to use for giving presentations when I travel—some of the newer units are compact and light enough to carry on a plane. A spacious advertisement in *USA Today* drew my attention: "We provide smart features that can save you even more money down the line. Want full specs? Just give us a ring." At the bottom of the page was a toll-free number.

I called and inquired into some of the product specifications. "I don't have that kind of information," the employee replied. "Would you like to talk with one of our technical reps?" After being transferred and put on hold for several minutes, the technical representative told me, "I'm kind of new here and am not sure what those exact specifications are. Would you like me to send you one of our technical brochures? Have you by chance looked at our Web site? It may have some information that will answer your question." "No," I replied, "I think I will move on." I declined to mention that the only reason I called was to save time by quickly obtaining technical information about the product over the phone, which they had promised in the advertisement.

Delivering on the Promise to Customers

A competing organization with proficient workers would put this company out of business. The worker who answered the call not only would be able to deliver the promised information to the customer, but also would leave the indelible impression that this was an organization that delivered on its promises to customers. When customers have so many options in choosing providers, any gap between what has been promised and what is delivered will provoke most customers to switch. Survival for any company today hinges on the connection between the promise made to customers and the ability of the work force to deliver on that promise.

Consider the following four questions to establish a framework for understanding the relationship between the promise you make to customers and the ability, or *proficiency*, that your workers need in order to deliver on that promise.

First, *what promises are made to your customers?* Seek and find the commitments and promises that have been made to your customers. This discovery is often called the "value proposition" and should focus squarely on the customer.

Second, *what role do your people play in delivering on that promise?* Very few promises are fulfilled without the critical involvement of people. In a business that offers intangible services, every promise is fulfilled by a person; the personal service *is* the product. A deep understanding of how effective your employees currently are in fulfilling the promise to the customer is the first step in identifying what development and learning efforts will be required for them to truly succeed.

Third, *which of your competitors makes a similar promise?* The truth is that when you compare value propositions, marketing collateral, and service offerings, there's often a remarkable similarity among products and services in today's market.

Finally, *what happens if your competition delivers on that promise first?* This is the critical organizing question for those who choose to compete with both speed and proficiency. Simply asking this question will inspire a series of conversations about the ability of your workforce to do battle. This inquiry will also cause significant anxiety as you ponder your vulnerability to a nimble, proficient competitor.

Today's business environment demands a new perspective on employee development—a shift from traditional education-as-training-event to education that on every level augments the delivery of value to customers. In the future, this focus will be a fundamental driver of competitiveness in a firm. The time a worker spends in any form of learning must be tied *directly* to the promises made to customers. When the connection is tight, learners immediately understand their role in delivering value to the customer, and the objective of learning and performing is literally defined by what the organization is attempting to do for its customer.

What Is the Proficiency Threshold?

This book uses the term *proficiency* to describe the ability of an individual worker to produce value for customers. It is critical to distinguish proficiency from the objective of traditional training, the acquisition of knowledge. Proficiency requires doing, application, and results. Knowledge, the end product of most training, is by itself inadequate; knowledge alone will not enable an employee

43

to perform. A person can attain knowledge, even advanced knowledge, and still be unable to perform satisfactorily to meet a customer's need. Think of fresh college graduates entering the job market with heads full of recently acquired knowledge: few will be able to immediately step into an assignment and begin to add value. The same is true of any worker who has attended a lecture or read a book. Of course, proficiency requires knowledge, but it also requires that the knowledge come alive through experience. Proficiency is a more potent objective than training and knowledge creation: proficiency is the use of knowledge in action for the purpose of producing value for a customer.

The *proficiency threshold*, therefore, *is the exact moment when a worker can convert knowledge through action into the promised value for the customer.* The proficiency reached at this moment can be measured, and it can't be faked. Defining the precise moment when a worker can perform well enough to deliver the promised value to customers is the crucial action for an organization to execute on its competitive strategy.

For individual employees, the proficiency threshold is the moment at which both they and the organization know that value can be delivered to customers. At first glance that may seem obvious, but think how often businesses seem confused about what proficiency their employees need in order to serve customers. For an example, all we have to do is return to Kyle, the technician at US West. In that situation, my vision of the problem-solving skills needed by frontline workers had little or nothing to do with the problems they actually faced in serving customers. The threshold level of proficiency is crucial to competitive advantage because it is the point at which an employee begins to contribute value in a particular job or task.

The point at which workers *together* can create and deliver value to the customer, the collective proficiency threshold, is the moment when the business' strategy and plans become executed. The proficiency threshold is reached when the sales and marketing team can sell and advertise value to customers with confidence, when orders are filled on time, when services meet customer expectations, and when the management team is leading as envisioned. By definition, the proficiency threshold links an individual worker to the vision and strategy of the organization in the context of his or her performance.

A key point here is that not all jobs in an organization require the same level of proficiency; the threshold level of proficiency depends on the position and the task at hand. Rarely would a senior sales manager, for example, need to have the technical financial proficiency of an accounting specialist. In this area, the manager probably needs to be proficient only in using sales reporting systems. Conversely, an accounting specialist need only understand the basic principles of the corporate sales strategy, whereas a senior manager needs to know the minute details of that strategy.

The fastest method to get the collective organization to the proficiency threshold, therefore, is to clearly identify the level of proficiency each person must achieve to deliver on the company's promise to the customer. The proficiency threshold may in fact be at one of three different levels, depending on the role of the employee: literacy, fluency, or mastery.

The time a worker spends in any form of learning must be tied *directly* to the promises made to customers.

Literacy is the ability to articulate knowledge in the context of one's job. This is the level usually attained during well-designed training events. For certain jobs, literacy may be the threshold level of proficiency—the accountant mentioned above, for example, is proficient if he understands the corporate sales strategy at the level of literacy—but for most primary tasks in most jobs, it is insufficient.

Fluency is the ability to perform a task with ease. It can be attained only through actual practice and application. It is a function of the amount of experience accumulated over a period of time. Fluency marks the threshold level of proficiency required for the essential functions of most jobs, and yet the vast majority of traditional training activities do not ensure that learners reach this level.

Mastery is achieved with additional experience, when one acquires true expertise. This level is seldom reached because it is generally beyond what is necessary to deliver value to customers, and therefore more experienced employees are promoted to jobs requiring greater skills before they master the skills of their previous job. But for certain jobs, fluency may not be enough and mastery may represent threshold proficiency.

By identifying the proficiency threshold for each critical task of each position in an organization, decision makers take the first step toward formulating a precise strategy to develop the workforce faster. This allows them to determine how best to use time and financial resources to achieve the crucial initial level of performance. In this process, proficiency across an organization is viewed strategically rather than tactically.

Threshold Proficiency in Action

Let's take as an example a division of a company that offers products for the home office market—computer hard drives, printers, modems, memory, and monitors—and is launching a new series of products and services and needs to train its people. Traditionally, a course would be designed to train the sales and marketing group, and anything and everything that might need to be learned would be stuffed into this one course. In essence, the course would be designed to bring the average sales and marketing employee to a level of mastery in one lengthy mass session—a vain effort that would barely make the employee literate and will leave the organization with a sales force that will not reach the level of proficiency needed to perform effectively in front of skeptical customers. Figures 3.1 and 3.2 illustrate the typical expectations and typical results of this approach.

Expectations of Traditional Sales Training

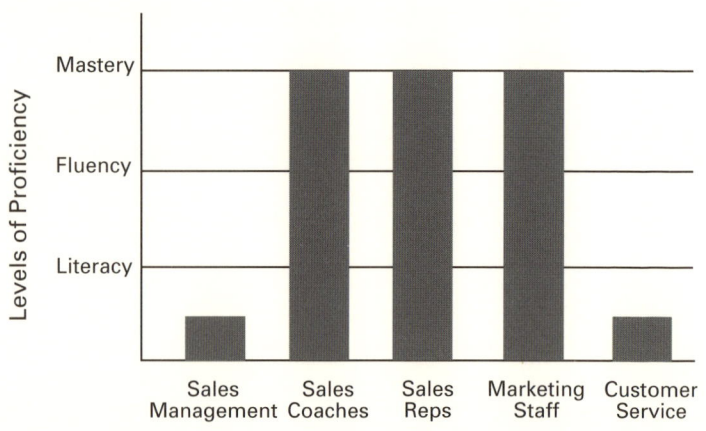

Figure 3.1

Results of Traditional Sales Training

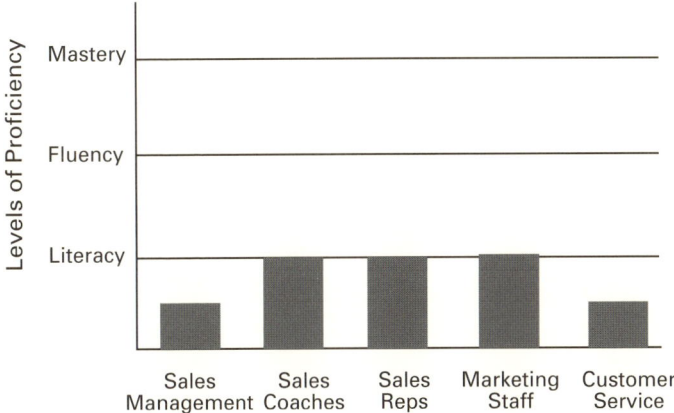

Figure 3.2

In contrast, through strategic identification of the threshold level of proficiency, an organization not only can bring its sales and marketing employees to proficiency more quickly but can finally include the other important functions necessary for the successful introduction of new products and services. Figure 3.3 illustrates the strategy of threshold proficiency this company. Not only are resources applied more strategically, but workers begin reaching the literacy level very quickly, in a myriad of ways made possible by today's advancements in technology. In addition, very few employees will need to achieve mastery by the completion of the first training efforts. Only the sales coaches and mentors (about 5 percent of the total group) need to reach the mastery level as their initial threshold. Most members of the sales and marketing team need to reach a fluency level, and they can achieve this with a much shorter course than traditional

Breakaway

training, followed by rapid rounds of practice. Sales management, customer service, administrative support, and legal staff need to achieve varying levels of proficiency.

Strategically Selecting the Proficiency Threshold

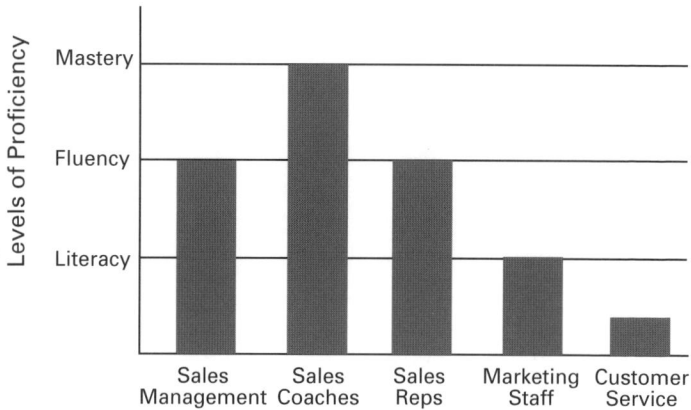

Figure 3.3

Threshold Proficiency and the Value Chain

In their book *The Balanced Scorecard*, Robert Kaplan and David Norton define a common set of attributes that organize value propositions in all industries. These propositions fall into three categories: product and service, image, and relationships.[1] As shown in Figure 3.4, these attributes help map how the value proposition relates to the worker. This map helps decision makers understand—in many cases for the first time—the relationship between the organization's proposition of value to the customer and the true proficiency needs of the worker.

Linking the Value Proposition to the Worker

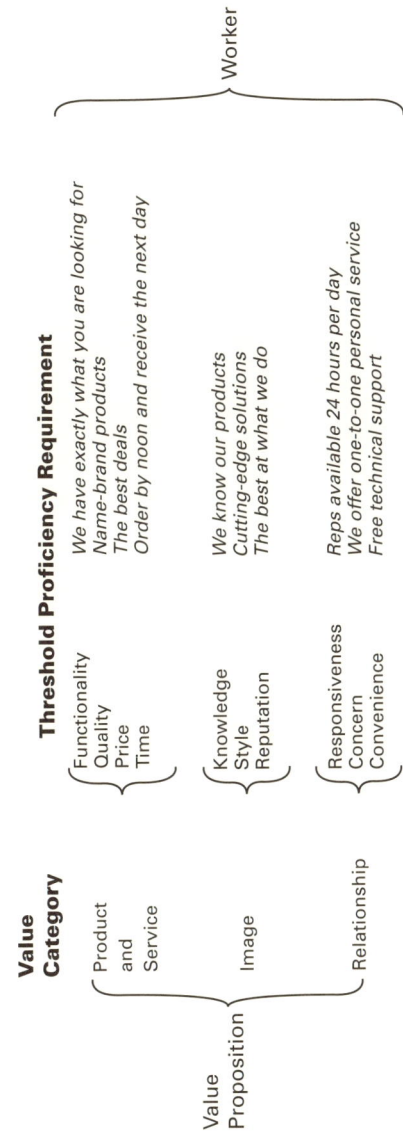

Figure 3.4

The proficiency threshold is the exact moment when a worker can convert knowledge through action into the promised value for the customer. Defining the proficiency threshold is the crucial action for an organization to execute on its competitive strategy.

Take, for example, the home office solution company discussed earlier. Its value propositions to potential consumers fit into these three categories. Failure to deliver in any one of the categories because of a nonproficient work force will leave this organization vulnerable to the competition and could undermine any chance of building a long-term relationship with a customer.

Let's take one possible promise to customers in the product and service category as an example: *"Order by noon and receive your product the next day."* Assuming that the fast turnaround strategy of a company in this market is correct and the value proposition will set the company apart from the competition, the leaders can now look directly at the proficiency threshold needed by the workforce to deliver on this promise. The easiest way to do this is to clearly understand the specific process within the organization that creates value for a customer. Linking the steps of this process builds what is known as the value chain. In this example, the value chain has four significant links, shown in Figure 3.5. Each of these functions in the company will be involved in delivering on this promise to customers.

The Value Chain

Order by noon and receive your products the next day

| Procurement, Inventory Management | Sales, Marketing, Customer Service | Shipping, Packaging | Technical Support & Service |

Figure 3.5

Breakaway

The Value Chain and Threshold Proficiency

Value Proposition: Order by Noon and Receive your Products the Next Day

Links in the Value Chain	Performance Requirement	Threshold Proficiency
STEPS IN THE PROCESS OF DELIVERING ON THE PROMISE	WHAT MUST BE ACCOMPLISHED TO DELIVER ON THE PROMISE	THE INITIAL LEVEL OF PROFICIENCY AT WHICH THE WORKER CAN DELIVER ON THE PROMISE
Procurement Inventory Management	Available inventory Accurate inventory management systems	*Buyer/Procurement Specialist* LITERACY • Customer ordering process • Marketing events and activity • Shipping and packaging methods FLUENCY • Usage of Inventory Management System • Purchasing process/guidelines • Quality assurance and warranty feedback system
Sales Marketing Customer Service Toll-free support system	Precise order placement	*Sales and Service Representative* LITERACY • Shipping and packaging process • Active listening FLUENCY • Order fulfillment system/product selection, service and pricing • Inventory Management System
Shipping and Packaging	Accurate inventory management system Efficient warehouse retrieval process High quality and efficient packaging process Quick turnaround with overnight delivery company	*Warehouse and Packaging Specialist* LITERACY • Order Fulfillment System • Inventory Management System FLUENCY • Warehouse automated retrieval system (part numbering schema) • Packaging quality standards and process • Delivery process with UPS, FedEx, Airborne
Technical Service and Support	Development of specific packaging and shipping requirements and instructions	*Technical Service Representative* LITERACY • Order Fulfillment System FLUENCY • Vendor technical requirements (storage and packaging) • Customer feedback and complaints (unpacking)

Table 3.1

Starting with the proposition of fast turnaround (order by noon and receive products the next day), the proficiency threshold for each link of the value chain can now be clearly identified. One of the biggest advantages with this approach is that it allows the workforce to understand how their proficiency will deliver value to the customer and build barriers for the competition. The relationship between the value proposition, the customer, and the worker becomes abundantly clear.

Table 3.1 illustrates the performance requirements and proficiency threshold definitions for each link in this value chain. The organizational proficiency threshold is reached by having proficient workers throughout the delivery process. A weak link will result in the delivery of a potentially weak product or service. In this example, decision makers need to assess the individual value proposition and its importance to the overall business strategy. Taking the time to lay out the threshold definitions for this proposition will, in essence, force a set of priorities on the leaders. The organizational proficiency threshold required to make sure a customer can "order by noon and receive products the next day" can seem daunting. And this proposition is only one of ten made to customers through their marketing and sales efforts. The number of value propositions this organization can deliver to the marketplace—and how fast it can do this—is a function of its proficiency and the clarity of its business strategy.

Obviously, focusing on only one value proposition highlights a narrow view of the actual threshold requirements for a worker in this value chain. Examining the sum of the requirements for meeting each of the propositions through-

out the delivery process reveals the proficiency requirements for the entire organization and for all workers in that
organization. You can see the beginning of this analysis for
this company in Table 3.1. Each worker will then know the
definition of his or her minimal proficiency requirements in
the three categories of value delivery. This understanding,
for both the worker and the decision maker, creates a
momentum of learning activity that is directed toward the
customer. Any training event outside this target will slow
the speed in which the worker can become proficient
enough to provide value to the customer.

Threshold Proficiency and the Back Office

Every position in an organization provides value to customers—even supporting personnel through their interac-
tions with "internal customers." Quick turnaround of
action items and project commitments, thorough research,
well-tested designs, and accurate data are all examples of
the value propositions that employees give to each other
every day in the operation of a business. These are critical
to the success of any operation and should be treated just
like value propositions to customers in terms of threshold
proficiency. This is consistent with Dr. W. Edwards
Deming's notion that in internal customer-supplier relationships, the next person in the process should be treated
as a customer.[2] Deming wrote at length the importance of
never passing along a defect to a fellow employee,
because it will obstruct the next step in the process and
will eventually find its way to the customer. The defect in

this case could be slow, non-responsive service, dated information, or high labor costs. Each component in the value chain must increase customer value, not subtract from it. In most cases, every department, from the finance department to facilities management to industrial engineering and information technologies support groups, have a sweeping impact on the value chain. This is why a definition of internal threshold levels of proficiency must be developed.

A worker who supplies value to the internal processes must have the same understanding of the business strategy and value proposition as does a worker who directly affects the delivery of a product or service to an external customer. It is essential that support staff understand their own contributions to the final value delivered to a customer. They then perceive themselves as instrumental in the overall vision and mission of the company. Organizations that have developed proficiency threshold targets for support workers find that the method for developing them, is, in itself, a key tool for revealing the definition of value among support staff, who are usually far removed from the actual delivery to a customer. Figure 3.6 illustrates one internal value proposition for the cost management group of a mid-sized software development company in San Jose, California. It identifies for this company the specific value propositions in Kaplan and Norton's three categories: produce and service, image, and relationship.

By definition, the proficiency threshold links an individual worker to the vision and strategy of the organization in the context of his or her performance.

Internal Value Proposition

Product and Service	*Accurate weekly cost reports* *Accurate monthly operations report (actual to budget)*
Image	*Smart and competent financial managers*
Relationship	*Quick turn-around, responsive, and easy to work with*

Figure 3.6

As with the external value chain, the components of an internal value chain need to be described. In this case, the proposed value of an accurate monthly report is deemed crucial: an erroneous report could have serious consequences to the business and impact the external value chain leading to the customer. Therefore, those producing the needed report must reach threshold proficiency quickly. The components of the chain are shown in Figure 3.7.

Internal Value Chain

Accurate monthly operations report

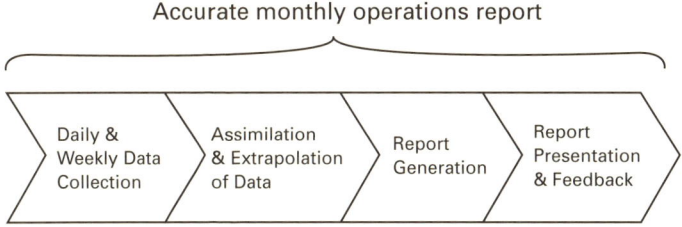

| Daily & Weekly Data Collection | Assimilation & Extrapolation of Data | Report Generation | Report Presentation & Feedback |

Figure 3.7

The Internal Value Chain and Threshold Proficiency

Value Proposition: Accurate Monthly Operations

Links in the Value Chain	Performance Requirement	Threshold Proficiency
STEPS IN THE PROCESS OF DELIVERING ON THE PROMISE	WHAT MUST BE ACCOMPLISHED TO DELIVER ON THE PROMISE	THE INITIAL LEVEL OF PROFICIENCY AT WHICH THE WORKER CAN DELIVER ON THE PROMISE
Daily and weekly data collection	Accurate collection process Timely collection method Collecting the correct data	*Cost Manager* LITERACY • Data collection procedures within the business processes FLUENCY • Usage of Cost Management System • Labor collection, Payables, Expenses Inventory Control, Contract Management
Assimilation and extrapolation of the data	Ensure that costs are allocated to the proper cost center, billed to the correct project and in the correct billing period. Analyze the causes for deviations from the forecast Check current operating assumptions with actual performance and suggest changes	*Cost Manager* FLUENCY • Cost allocation and billing codes • Forecast and operating assumptions • Performance metrics MASTERY • Operational analysis of cost overruns
Report generation	Development of an accurate and brief cost management report for the operation	*Cost Manager* FLUENCY • Report and presentation guidelines • PowerPoint software • Expectations of senior management

Table 3.2

Many support roles are performed by small groups of workers and often by a single person. In this example, the way the internal value chain is defined relative to the internal value proposition defines the proficiency threshold, not only for the cost management group, but for a single worker in that group. This definition of the value chain gives each worker an understanding of the proficiency requirements to deliver on their service. Consider the operational advantages of having a support worker linked to the rest of the business through a clear definition of what must be delivered and how much know-how is required to deliver it. Table 3.2 lays out the performance requirements and threshold proficiency definition for this cost management team.

Initiating the Breakaway

Delivering value to customers rapidly is made possible by building the basic capacity of an organization and its people to get their jobs done more quickly and effectively—to reach threshold levels of proficiency fast. A breakaway starts when you reach the proficiency threshold. Proficient workers become contributing team members; they produce innovative ideas; they work safely but quickly, they go on to achieve even greater levels of proficiency, and they win the race.

4

Accelerate the
Accumulation of Experience

The accumulation of experience is by far the most critical step in the learning process, yet the management of and investment in this phase is nearly always left to chance.

On a recent trip, I happened to be standing on the airport escalator behind a woman who was schlepping what seemed like enough luggage for four people. Coincidentally, she was seated next to me on the flight. She had been forced to check her largest bag but was adamant about carrying on three others and crowding them under the seats—hers and mine—and in the overhead compartment.

During the flight, she pulled out four bulging three-ring binders. For nearly an hour she wrestled with the binders, placing sticky notes on specific pages and jotting down reminders in the text. As our conversation developed, she explained that she was bound for New Jersey to facilitate a weeklong sales training class for her company.

"What do you expect out of your students after they attend the class?" I asked her. As if on cue, she turned to a tab in one of the binders, clipped open the rings, and handed me five neatly outlined sheets, each labeled "Learning Outcomes." There was one outline for every day of her course. It seemed to make sense until I looked closely at the outlines. Stuffed into five eight-hour training sessions was what must have been enough information for a full semester of a college marketing course. In one forty-hour training session, she would try to jam massive amounts of information into the brains of her students.

This was a classic example of contemporary corporate training—all things delivered in one session. Condensed schedules have forced designers to cram as much material and information as possible into the available time period, a reactive management response to perceived needs. Corporate educators usually have only one chance to work with their students, and they try to get through the greatest amount of material in the time they have.

How Workers Really Learn

The facilitator's plight forced me to reexamine my own thinking and the logic behind the current corporate training model.

Every day, thousands of employees from around the country are sent to similar five-day training in sales processes. The decision to send them assumes that all of them are at ground zero in their familiarity with the new concepts. And because nothing is planned to reinforce the information conveyed in the class once they are back on the job, it is additionally assumed that they will *automatically* be better, more productive salespeople immediately following the training. Even more farfetched is the assumption that salespeople will gladly give up five days of potential commissions because they seek the immediate benefits that will result from taking the class. These misguided and false training assumptions become an enormous obstacle to the organization's ability to learn faster—if learning takes place at all.

It is time to use this past century's research on human learning to understand how we have strayed and to find our path to the future. We know from nearly nine decades of research about adult learning that humans do not learn without a natural progression from discovery through experience. Three thinkers in particular have informed our understanding of this fact.

John Dewey, an educator born during the Civil War, was truly one of the pioneers of inquiry into human thought and learning. His research at the University of Chicago and later at Columbia is the seminal work on the human as a learner and a performer. His book *How We Think*, published early last century, serves as a springboard for understanding the training of the human mind. Dewey draws a strong distinction between the acquisition of *information* and the application of *practice* and *thinking*, with the latter being the only true way for a human to learn. "There is all the difference in the world when the acquisition of information is treated as an end in itself, or is made an integral portion of the training of thought. *The assumption that information which has been accumulated apart from the use in the recognition and solution of a problem may later on be freely employed at will by thought is quite false.* The skill acquired with the aid of intelligence, the only information which, otherwise than by accident, can be put to logical use, is that acquired in the course of thinking while experiencing. Because their knowledge has been achieved in connection with the needs of specific situations, men of little book-learning are often able to put to effective use every ounce of knowledge they possess; while men of vast erudition are often swamped by the mere bulk of their learning, because memory, rather than experience, has been the operative in obtaining it."[1]

Another researcher who has contributed greatly to the understanding of human learning is Robert Gagné, arguably the forefather of instructional design. During his five decades of research, Gagné produced a framework for linking human learning with a process for instruction. Table 4.1, adapted from a paper he published in 1970, highlights this relationship.[2] Gagné contended that instruction must be integrated with four natural learning processes. The *introductory phase* sets the stage for learning by engaging the student's interest and attention. The *initial guidance phase* supports the initial learning by giving directions, suggestions, and prompts. The *application phase* is directed at retrieval, with the aim of retention. And finally, the *performance and feedback phase* is targeted at creating situations for student performance by providing feedback relevant to that performance. Gagné's work holds that learners progress through all four learning processes on their way to achieving a new level of performance; if instruction is intended to advance a learner's performance, it must be designed to take a learner all the way to the fourth phase, *performance and feedback.*

Learning Processes and Phases of Instruction

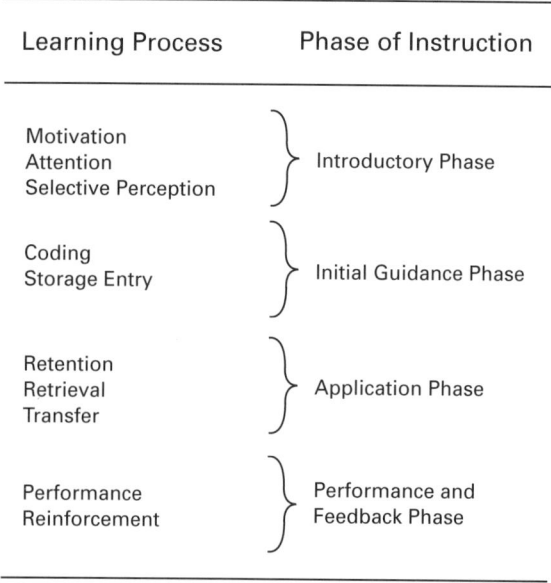

Learning Process	Phase of Instruction
Motivation Attention Selective Perception	Introductory Phase
Coding Storage Entry	Initial Guidance Phase
Retention Retrieval Transfer	Application Phase
Performance Reinforcement	Performance and Feedback Phase

Table 4.1

Finally, the recent work of John R. Anderson on the
integration of learning and memory divides how skills
develop into three stages, using as an example the act of
learning how to shift gears with a manual transmission.[3]
In the initial act of learning, called the *cognitive stage*, the
learner works from a set of instructions or observations. A
student driver, for example, is exposed to the principles of
a standard transmission and sees a demonstration. In the
second stage, called the *associative stage*, the skill makes a
transition from a declaration to a procedure. The learner
in this stage begins to experiment with the instructions.
For instance, the student driver learns to coordinate the
releasing of the clutch with the application of the gas
pedal so as to not kill the engine. Finally, a learner pro-
gresses to the *autonomous stage*, where the skill becomes
repeated in an automated and rapid fashion. In this stage,
cognitive involvement is gradually eliminated—it
becomes second nature. Most drivers advancing to this
stage do not even realize a separate relationship between
the clutch, the gas pedal, and the stick shift. Anderson
concludes that as a skill becomes more practiced, it under-
goes dramatic changes, including great reductions in its
cognitive involvement; hence improved performance
requires a learner to reach the autonomous stage.

The Real-World Learning Process

These thinkers have contributed greatly to the understanding of learning and the human mind. Sadly, few of their
conclusions are known and applied consistently outside of
academia. To build a bridge between this landmark
research and the daily challenges of business leaders, I

We know from nearly nine

decades of research about

adult learning that humans

do not learn without a

natural progression from

discovery through

experience.

have attempted to link these key principles and theories to the everyday practice and language of today's business environment. During the course of research for this book, I observed companies creating new learning for workers to reach the proficiency threshold and deliver value to customers fast. I identified four phases in this real-world learning process, culminating in the accumulation of experience and increased performance. These four phases are:

- Phase 1: *Introduction* to new information
- Phase 2: *Assimilation* of the newly acquired information with previous knowledge and experience
- Phase 3: *Translation* of the new information combined with past experience into specific knowledge
- Phase 4: *Accumulation of experience* through practice, trial and error, and feedback on performance

Let's look at these in greater detail. The first phase requires the *introduction* of new information. The learner must be exposed to a new set of data to initiate the process. Information comes to us in endless variety of forms and through a myriad of media every day. Capturing the learner's attention requires that this information be new and different. In the training process I am describing, this phase is finished in a very short period of time.

In the second phase, the learner *assimilates* the new data with previous knowledge and experience. It is during this phase that a learner passes judgment about whether the new information or potential new skill has real benefit. The learner asks, "What's in it for me?" and the answer either activates or suppresses interest in learning.

Few people can both consume new information *and* change their performance or behavior immediately. So in the third phase, learners reflect on the new information and *translate* it into the world in which they work—to place the information in the context of their jobs and thus to understand how it fits. Without going through the process of translation, a learner is only *informed* and can rarely make the leap to any form of application or practice.

Let's pause to reflect on these three stages. At this point, the prospective learner is versed in and has contextual knowledge of the subject matter. In the industry vernacular, "training and development" is the sum of phase 1 and phase 2 and, occasionally, part of phase 3. In other words, once they have gone this far, learners in traditional training are assumed to have been "trained." Evaluations of well-designed training sessions include such questions as: "Will the information gained from this course help you perform better in your job?" and "As a result of this course, can you better describe why we need to continually improve the service to our customers?" Good scores or positive answers to these questions lead one to believe that the training has been effective, but training by this definition is only a fraction of the learning process.

That's because the most important learning occurs in the fourth and most time-consuming phase, when knowledge is transformed into practice through an *accumulation of experience* using the new knowledge. The learning is not complete until experience is accumulated and the proficiency threshold is reached. The accumulation of experience is by far the most critical step in the learning process, yet the management of and investment in this phase is nearly always left to chance. Although the accumulation of experience requires time and resources many times greater than that required for the first three phases, these resources are rarely budgeted, and the accumulation of experience generally occurs by accident, not design.

It is critical that we grasp the implications of this oversight. If the accumulation of experience is not managed, it does still occur on the job, but it costs much more in time and money than if it had been designed. The costs are reflected in lost sales, lost customers, employee turnover, overtime, accidents, scrap and rework, and disappointing improvements in productivity.

Accumulation of Experience Left to Chance

An example from the telecommunications industry will help drive home this point. The Internet revolution has been made possible by the conversion of our communications infrastructure from copper wire to fiber-optic cables made of tiny strands of glass. The telecommunications industry has an aching shortage of workers who can connect, or *splice*, these glass cables. Across the country, fiber-optic cables sit, waiting to be spliced; the lack of skilled workers has become a significant bottleneck in the conversion process. In the new world of telecommunications, this shortage alone can be responsible for a company's failure to compete, while those companies who get their workers to proficiency fast will enjoy an enormous advantage against their competition.

It typically takes eight weeks—forty working days—for an experienced copper splicer to become proficient in splicing the tiny glass cables. The training begins with a classroom lecture from an instructor who *introduces* the differences between copper and glass splicing, the placement of the fiber cable, the engineering requirements for

73

Breakaway

The traditional training model
ignores completely the need
for learners to accumulate
experience, and therefore,
accumulation proceeds at its
own pace, generally driven
by various emergencies.

quality of the connection and conductivity, and the special safety requirements for working with microscopic pieces of glass. The student *assimilates* the new information with previous experience splicing copper wire. At the end of the first week, the classroom information is placed into a three-ring binder and carried into the next week's lab work, in which for three days the learner uses the precision tools required to laser weld two extremely thin pieces of glass together. In this phase, the learner goes from being a copper splicer who twists two pieces of wire together with a nut to a fiber-optic splicer who uses sophisticated tools to connect glass strands. The new information and past experience are *translated* into new knowledge.

In a questionnaire submitted at the end of the class, typically more than 90 percent of the students agree that they have enough new knowledge and know-how to splice fiber-optic cable. But workers aren't yet ready to deliver on the promise made to customers. Up to this point, workers have learned in a controlled environment. Following the class, however, some of the splicers are needed for other work and are not available for splicing work for a number of weeks; their road to proficiency is difficult because of memory decay following the class. Those who go directly to work in splicing jobs encounter all sorts of new situations—deep, muddy excavations; water-filled service holes; broken cable that is fractured at random points, contaminated with dirt, or otherwise touched by Mother Nature in ways not anticipated in the classroom. The learner must adapt classroom knowledge to the real problems found in the field. At this point, and only at this point, does a worker even *begin* to cross the

Learning Process in Traditional Training and Development

Total Time to Reach Proficiency Threshold

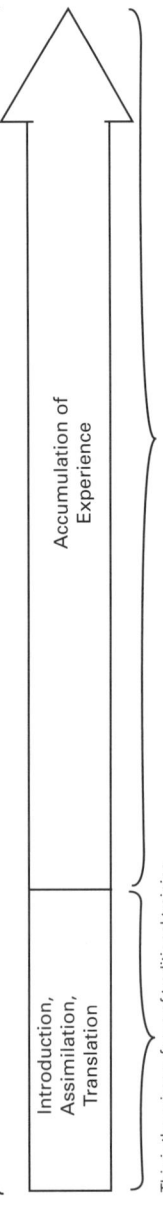

Introduction, Assimilation, Translation

Accumulation of Experience

This is the primary focus of traditional training and development—tightly managed and carefully measured

This phase is usually left to chance and may take many weeks or months to complete

Figure 4.1

Learning Process that Focuses on Accelerating the Accumulation of Experience

Total Time to Reach Proficiency Threshold

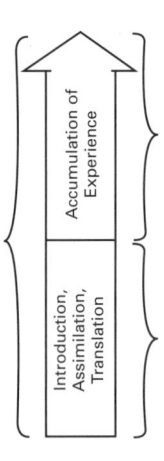

Introduction, Assimilation, Translation

Accumulation of Experience

This is often converted to self-study or short bursts of classroom learning to prepare for practice

This phase is managed with closely monitored practice sessions

Figure 4.2

bridge to the proficiency threshold by *accumulating experience* with the new knowledge.

From the beginning of training, it took an average of eight weeks before the worker could deliver on the promise to customers (Figure 4.1). Of these eight weeks, only the first two were budgeted, managed, designed, and measured. In the following six weeks, the worker's attempt to gain enough experience to splice fiber optics was not only left to chance, but was also fraught with potential inconsistencies and bad habits formed through the random learning process. The traditional training model assumes that at the end of a training event, a worker will immediately have the knowledge and ability to perform more effectively. It ignores completely the need for learners to accumulate experience, and therefore, accumulation proceeds at its own pace, generally driven by various emergencies. Some employees never reach proficiency; others achieve it only through trial and error, practicing on real customers. By managing the accumulation of experience and the rate at which it occurs, managers can reduce dramatically the time it takes to create proficient employees.

Managing the Accumulation of Experience

What if an organization could reduce the time it took to reach threshold proficiency by managing the accumulation of experience instead of leaving it to chance? What if an organization could get its workers to the point where they could meet customers needs much faster than the competition—in this case, in *three weeks* instead of eight? Fortunately, there is an approach that differs from current practice, one that offers organizations huge competitive advantages.

Let's take as an example a telecommunications company that has recently decided to manage the accumulation of experience and so has dramatically reduced the time it takes to deliver value to the customer. Here's how they did it: The organization decided that after the classroom training, the expert training instructors would accompany their students into the field. Their new role as field coaches: to go on the job with a group of six workers and coach them until each could splice an entire cable of 144 hair-thin fiber-optic lines unassisted. When all six employees pass this test, the instructors receive another group of six learners. "I traded my wingtips for boots and it changed my life overnight," one coach said.

The field learning followed a classic model: The expert would demonstrate splicing under real-world conditions, with the learners watching and asking questions. Then the learners would splice, and the expert would provide immediate, personalized feedback. Learning and work were made one and the same. A majority of the training budget was redirected to the accumulation of experience, enabling workers to reach threshold proficiency in three weeks instead of eight and greatly increasing the organization's capacity to meet customers' needs. Figure 4.2 illustrates this change in approach.

In the end, it is the accumulation of experience that affords the most opportunity to reduce the cycle time it takes to become proficient and to gain significant competitive advantage. Managing the rapid accumulation of experience offers the biggest opportunity to shorten the cycle time to proficiency. Period.

Measure the
Cycle Time to Proficiency

Cycle time to proficiency threshold is a metric that will fundamentally change the planning, budgeting, and behavior of those charged with the overall competence of an organization's work force.

In the early 1980s I worked for a seasoned supervisor who also moonlighted as an industrial engineering professor at a local community college. As one might imagine, he was nuts about process measurement and statistical process control. His favorite mantra was "what gets measured gets done." He didn't originate the phrase, of course, but he was clearly someone who understood the relationship between process, measurement, and worker behavior. I have come to appreciate the wisdom in his teaching.

Take, for example, the proverbial "butts-in-seats" measurement of training success practiced by many organizations. This metric drives the training manager to build and maintain elaborate scheduling systems for routing workers into classes. It directs instructional designers to think in terms of "instructional days" and encourages savvy workers to build up a mountain of hours in their training transcripts. In turn, decision makers, witnessing more workers completing more hours of training, become complacent in their judgment of the education system and assume it is working. Ironically, most would agree that the number of people attending a course has little relationship to how well they ultimately perform on the job, yet many organizations continue to use training hours as the ultimate metric for success or failure of learning programs.

A New Metric of Human Development

In order to increase the speed by which an organization can deliver on its value proposition, a new measure and a

Breakaway

Cycle Time in Traditional Training and Development

Total Time to Reach Proficiency Threshold
(193 days)

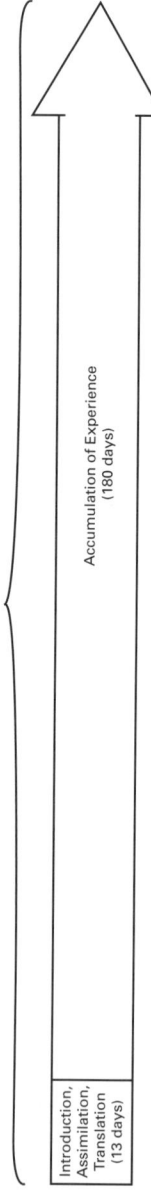

Introduction, Assimilation, Translation (13 days)

Accumulation of Experience (180 days)

Figure 5.1

Reduced Cycle Time by Focusing on Accumulation of Experience

Total Time to Reach Proficiency Threshold
(63 Days)

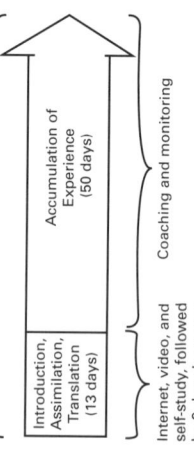

Introduction, Assimilation, Translation (13 days)

Accumulation of Experience (50 days)

Internet, video, and self-study, followed by 3-day classroom course

Coaching and monitoring

Figure 5.2

new perspective is needed. *Cycle time to proficiency thresh-old* is a metric that will fundamentally change the planning, budgeting, and behavior of those charged with the overall competence of an organization's work force.

Cycle time to proficiency threshold, unlike "butts in seats," is a measurement that is consistent with business practice that is already used across nearly all parts of an organization, aside from the training department. If the beginning and end points of a process can be defined and a clock or calendar is available, cycle time can be measured. Wasteful steps hidden in the daily operational system become illuminated when the objective of training is not to fill seats or produce instructional days, but rather to reduce the amount of time it takes each worker to become proficient and perform.[1] It is for this reason that improvements in execution speed follow cycle time measurement. Remember, "what gets measured gets done."

Measuring cycle time to proficiency threshold means measuring the process that occurs as a worker accumulates enough experience to provide value to the customer. The overall measure of cycle time to proficiency takes into account all time between the first learning event and the ultimate performance. Figure 5.1 illustrates the cycle time to proficiency threshold in a typical example of traditional training and development. After the initial learning event in which the worker goes through the process of introduction, assimilation, and translation of new material, the critical accumulation of experience is left to chance, and therefore the entire process of reaching the proficiency threshold may take six months or more.

As one can see, the proficiency threshold metric differs greatly from the standard practice of measuring a single event—such as 3-day classroom training—within the larger process. The key difference is that it measures the total time it takes for an individual to achieve the desired level of performance so that value can be delivered to customers.

This insight drives the decision makers of the organization to focus on steps in the learning process that will most dramatically reduce the overall cycle time. In the example in Figure 5.1, this is not the 3-day course nor the 13 days it takes for workers to complete all of the traditional training, but rather the 180 days needed to accumulate the experience necessary to perform at the threshold level. The cycle time to proficiency metric provides a panoramic view of a worker's path toward performance, producing the data needed to identify the resources that will quicken the pace. An astute leader, using the above example, would focus on the accumulation of experience phase, as it represents over 90 percent of the cycle time and the biggest area for improvement.

Many corporations around the globe are trying to reduce the time a worker spends in the classroom or attending a training event. If you seek a clear operational advantage, redirect your focus from further compressing the introduction, assimilation, and translation events, and instead apply innovation and resources to the accumulation of experience. Figure 5.2 illustrates that by accelerating the accumulation of experience, an organization can cut the cycle time to proficiency by two-thirds, saving more than one-hundred days per employee. This clearly outweighs the extreme effort required to reduce a three-day course to two days—a course that will still leave performers well short of the proficiency threshold.

Measuring the Proficiency Rate

In addition to measuring cycle time to proficiency for individuals, an organization must measure its *proficiency rate*—the speed by which the organization as a whole is able to deliver on the value proposition. Linking the average cycle time of individuals reaching proficiency with the total number of people needed to reach the threshold level will enable a leader to measure and monitor the entire organization's learning speed. This measurement is a kind of velocity, except that instead of being expressed in miles per hour or feet per second, this measurement of speed is expressed in terms of the number of people achieving the proficiency threshold in a defined period of time. "Hours in class" metrics only consider size of population and so offer no basis for competitive comparison, forecasting, or improvement. Nor can *individual* cycle time help organizations understand the complexities added, for example, by sheer numbers of people or limitations of infrastructure. This metric allows us to see learning not as simply a required event with no direct, measurable connection to the value proposition, but as a concrete, operational measure of business efficiency. The proficiency rate thus gives leaders flexibility because they can use it to make real-time decisions quickly. Both the effectiveness and the efficiency of training are measured with this new thinking, as shown in Table 5.1.

This metric allows us to see learning not as a compulsory event with no direct, measurable connection to the value proposition, but as a concrete, operational measure of business efficiency.

Proficiency Rate versus Traditional Quality Metrics

Traditional Measures	New Proficiency Metrics
Effectiveness	
Number of people in class	Number of people working to deliver on the value proposition
Number of total training hours	Cycle time to reach proficiency threshold
Efficiency	
Total training hours per person per year	The Proficiency Rate: Number of workers achieving proficiency threshold per day

Table 5.1

An organization's proficiency rate is calculated by taking the number of employees required to deliver on the value proposition and dividing this number by the average cycle time of workers reaching the threshold level:

$$\text{Organizational proficiency rate} = \frac{\text{Number of workers needed to deliver on the value proposition}}{\text{Current average cycle time to proficiency}}$$

The average is derived from a sample taken at strategic intervals as the targeted workforce continues down the developmental path. The result is a unit of proficiency for the organization over time—the number of proficient workers produced per day. Typical measurement intervals are weekly and often include an assessment, on-the-job performance criteria, and client feedback. Leaders can watch for overall improvement and trends that indicate that the accumulation of experience is improving as more workers reach the threshold level. The power of this metric comes not only from its simplicity, but from its ability to help leaders understand the rate at which their organization is changing. It clearly is not an absolute measure but rather an indicator of how fast an organization can reach its performance objectives. Each effort may have a different rate, as the number of people needed and the complexity of the task changes with each journey toward threshold proficiency.

To illustrate this measurement with a concrete example, let's turn to a global PCS provider currently undertaking the daunting task of moving 1,500 customer service representatives into a new call center in New Mexico. Each representative needs to be able to take a customer call, discover which PCS device (phone, pager, etc.) the customer has purchased, and establish the new service within a given time period while the customer remains on the call; this is their value proposition. Reaching the proficiency threshold requires each representative to go through a series of customer conversations aided by a coach in order to successfully establish the connection for the customer. The organizational proficiency rate after the first four weeks of this effort is measured according to our equation as follows:

$$\text{Organizational proficiency rate} = \frac{\text{1,500 customer service representatives}}{\substack{\text{27 average working days to} \\ \text{reach proficiency threshold} \\ \text{(30-employee sample)}}} = \substack{\text{55.5 proficient workers} \\ \text{produced per day}}$$

Over time, this organization will strive to increase this rate to over 70 workers per day by adding more coaches and having workers take less complex calls earlier in their learning process, thereby accumulating experience faster. Figure 5.2 highlights the ability of the proficiency rate to reveal improvement over time and to point out when progress has stalled.

Sample Organizational Proficiency Rate

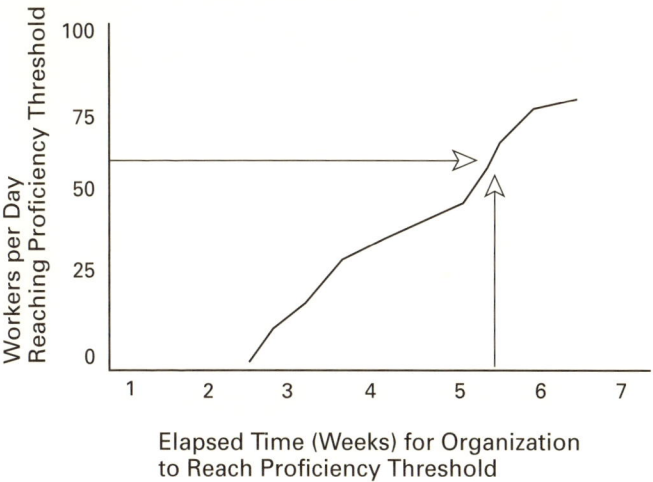

Figure 5.2

Revisiting the Learning Curve

Although the term *learning curve* is commonly used by people discussing training, I am often surprised by how poorly understood it is. In a recent presentation at the American Society for Training and Development conference, for example, a speaker kept referring to the "steep" learning curve in his organization. His implications of a tough climb and difficult individual battles with learning, however, showed how little he understood the concept. Once understood, this tool will help move leaders to make better and more timely decisions regarding the development of their people.

Learning curves were first employed in the airframe industry to forecast the labor savings that resulted from the accumulated experience of building one airframe after another. In essence, the technique links unit costs with volume and presumes that as cumulative unit volume increases, learning occurs and the costs per unit decline.[2]

Three key assumptions are used in learning curve theory:[3]

- The amount of time required to complete a given task will be less each time the task is undertaken
- Unit time will decrease at a decreasing rate
- This reduction in unit time will follow a predictable pattern

The airframe industry refined the theory to a relatively precise science using data from each successive performance. For example, if the assembly of plane Number 1 required 100,000 hours of labor, plane Number 2, 80,000 hours, plane Number 3, 64,000 hours, and so on, the organization is experiencing a 20 percent reduction in required labor following the assembly of each plane. This is considered an 80 percent learning curve. Note that the lower the percentage, the faster the learning.

The economies of the learning curve are realized through changes in learning rates and can have a dramatic effect on a company's overall competitiveness. As shown in Figure 5.3, for example, being able to learn only 5 percent faster can deliver a direct blow to a slower-learning competitor. In the sample case, a company with a learning curve of 85 percent has a cost-per-unit advantage of $13 (13 percent) over a company with a learning curve of 90 percent. The stark truth communicated through the learning curve is that proficiency and performance cannot be faked: the cost per unit improves only when output increases or input decreases.

Comparison of Learning Curve

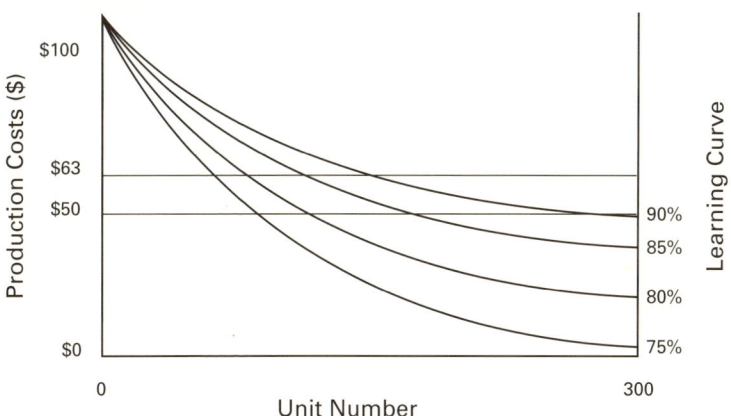

Figure 5.3

The number of units produced over a period of time can also be represented using the learning curve. This displays learning as a function of time and provides for a direct link to the cycle time to the proficiency threshold. Figure 5.4 represents the learning curve in units per day over time.

Learning Curve Represented in Units Per Day

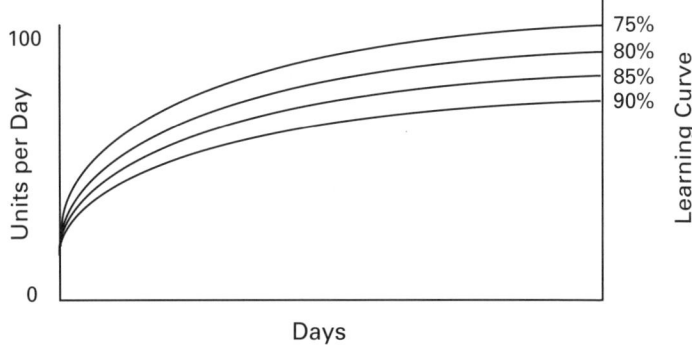

Figure 5.4

Financial analysts in manufacturing have traditionally been the biggest users of the learning curve, but don't be fooled by its manufacturing roots. Excuses for not using it in service industries include the elusive definition of a unit of service and the short life cycles of services. Take, for example, one of the many services now available that are customized for each customer. One could argue that a learning curve could not measure a customized service because the unit volume is only one. In fact, the opposite is true. Remember, the learning curve compares the cost components of a well-defined process against the experience or competence needed to successfully complete the steps within that particular process. The key to measuring productivity for service providers lies in identifying the knowledge and experience at the lowest level of detail, standardizing as many details as possible, and combining and mixing the details at the point of contact with the customer. World-class service providers know precisely the amount of time and cost required for each unit of service. ServiceMaster, for example, measures each unit of maintenance work; McDonalds, each unit of food preparation; US West, each telephone response; and United Parcel Service, each package delivered. These small and replicable units are the keys to effective capacity planning, work assignment, customer service, and competitive differentiation.[4] Therefore, learning-curve methodology applies to service organizations even more than to manufacturers. In a manufacturing system, it may take months to complete enough units to plot the learning curve. In a service environment, thousands of service units are produced daily, enabling a near-instant metric for learning.

Redefining the Learning Curve

Unfortunately, the learning curve is rarely applied in the emerging knowledge economy. Becoming the lowest-cost or highest-volume producer is only one dimension in an economy based on information, quality, and speed. Being the lowest-cost, lowest-priced producer may actually leave a company open for ambush by a competitor who can offer an equivalent product or service with more speed. Consumers continually remind us that they are willing to pay for speed. And a single-minded focus on unit-cost reduction might lead some decision makers to substitute capital improvements for people.[5] A powerful competitive metric therefore comes from predicting not only the unit costs over time, but also the time needed to get the organization to the point where it can deliver on the value proposition. The decision-making leverage

Learning-curve methodology

applies to service

organizations even more

than to manufacturers.

behind a more contemporary learning curve stems from the combination of the three human-dependent variables—quality, cycle time to the proficiency threshold, and cost. This new learning curve, which I call the *proficiency curve*, is illustrated in Figure 5.5.

The Proficiency Curve

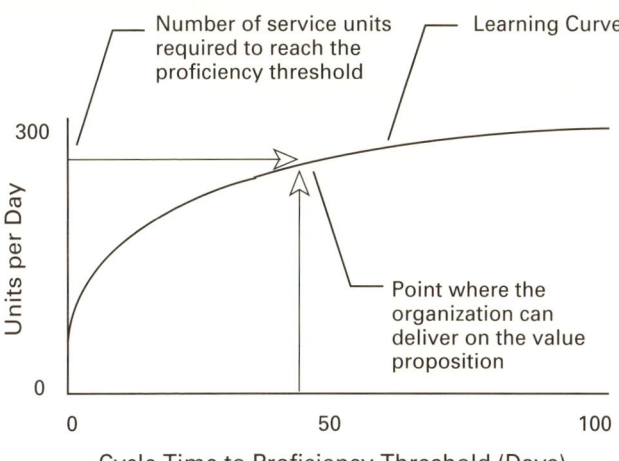

Figure 5.5

Consistent quality is delivered through a reliable process that quickly places workers at the threshold level of proficiency or beyond. *Time* is defined by the customers' demand for a product or service when they want it—a requirement dependent on the knowledge and proficiency of employees. Organizations that have employees at the threshold level of proficiency earlier in the life cycle of a product or service (shown with a proficiency curve) clearly can compete in the time dimension—both in speed to market and in maturity and sophistication of service. Therefore, the rate by which an organization reaches the proficiency threshold dictates its ability to compete in three dimensions: quality of service, service delivery time, and overall unit cost. The proficiency curve will enable decision makers to see all three variables plotted over time.

Applying the Proficiency Curve: The Partners of Starbucks

Recently, while I was giving a speech to a group of investors interested in the education industry, one gentleman challenged the notion of competing with proficient workers: "Tell me of a company that actually operates in this manner," he said. Good question. Here's my answer: To understand how speed to proficiency actually works to redirect decisions regarding the development of people, we only need to look to a company that I admire greatly, Starbucks. I am not only a devout shareholder, but also a frequent consumer of their services. Over the course of this past year, I have had many interviews with the employees, or *partners*, of Starbucks around the world. In 1987, Starbucks operated 11 stores and had 100 employees. They recently exceeded 2,600 retail locations with a 30 percent top-line improvement over last year. This places the company at about $550 million and growing.

Howard Schultz, CEO of Starbucks and author of *Pour Your Heart Into It*, has an undying passion for the continual proficiency of each partner in the Starbucks family. Even though nearly two-thirds of all partners are part-time employees, they are the heart and soul of the company. This stems from Schultz's understanding that "every dollar earned passes through their hands."[6] The proficiency threshold for the retail partners is a level of performance that results in superior customer service— service that will bring customers back to Starbucks. From Sydney to Toronto, each new partner clearly understands this proposition.

Each partner hired to work in a retail capacity at Starbucks receives a minimum of 25 hours of training during the first two to four weeks with the company. This includes substantial training in customer service skills, coffee knowledge, and drink-making techniques. As explained by a team of enthusiastic partners of a Denver barista, "We continue to practice on ourselves after the training—which is how we get really good!"[7] By the fourth week, they are fluent in the daily operational details of the store. They know how to gain the respect of customers, no matter their mood, and they can quickly create any drink on the menu within tight quality standards for temperature, texture, and flavor, and they can operate the computer cash register and explain to a customer the difference between the two major types of coffee beans and the effect roasting has on them. Those who reach a mastery level of proficiency in these tasks—on purpose—become the mentors and teachers for the next generation of partners.

Even as retail partners are reaching their proficiency threshold, non-retail employees (for example, accountants) reach a literacy level of proficiency in retail tasks by working for a few days each quarter in a store or roasting plant. Given this level of attention to employee proficiency, perhaps we should not be surprised that Starbucks is far ahead of the competition in employee loyalty. Nationwide, retailers and fast-food chains have an annual turnover rate ranging from 150 to 400 percent per year. Turnover at the average Starbucks barista ranges from 60 to 65 percent per year.[8]

Many partners attribute some of this success to the unique benefits package given to nearly all part-time partners. The ability to quickly bring delight to a customer, however, is a significant part of the generous benefits package. In general, partners perceive *their* value in the overall success of Starbucks (in the terms of this book, they understand their role in delivering value to the customer) very early in their employment—the first few weeks.

Starbucks clearly competes on the basis of the proficiency of its partners. In less than three weeks (their average cycle time to proficiency threshold), the training process produces an employee who can deliver high-quality service to customers. Not only can Starbucks deliver that service very quickly, but it clearly has competitive margins based on reaching operational effectiveness and efficiency *fast*.

If you are ready and willing to compete with Starbucks, here is your benchmark: I estimate the cycle time to proficiency for a retail partner at Starbucks to be between two and three working weeks, call it thirteen days. For every 1,000 partners, Starbucks' proficiency rate is 77 proficient partners per day.[9] During the first few days working in a barista, the average person serves between 80 and 100 customers per day, according to the energetic new partners I interviewed. Of course, this rate improves greatly over time and varies by retail location. Thus, formal training augmented by coaching in the barista brings a retail partner to proficiency threshold after serving approximately 600 customers. Additionally, each time a partner repeats the cycle of making a specific drink or operating the cash register, he or she does so approximately 10 percent faster than the previous time, netting a 90 percent learning curve. Figures 5.6 and 5.7 represent the relationship of these metrics.

Starbucks' Proficiency Rate

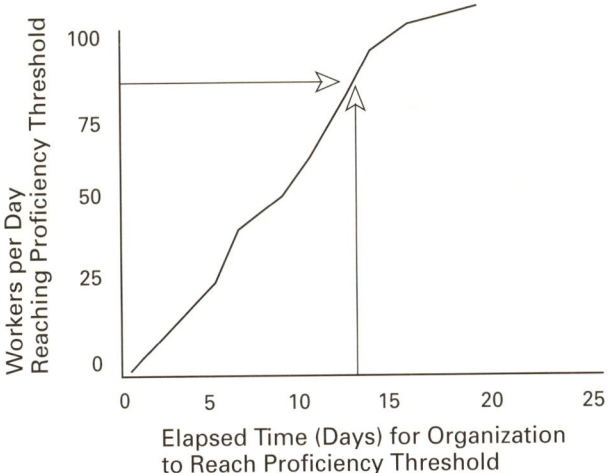

Figure 5.6

Starbucks' Proficiency Curve

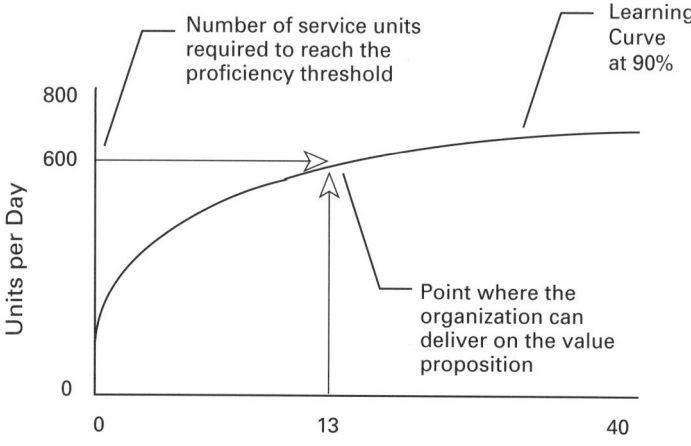

Figure 5.7

Compared to others in the fast-food retailing market, Starbucks has outpaced its competitors by clearly understanding the importance of quickly getting its partners to the threshold level of performance. While competitors (often located next door to Starbucks) struggle to retain the basic level of service, Starbucks entices its many proficient partners to organize poetry readings with customers, introduce local art and ideas, and move the customer "experience" to yet another level.

Staying Grounded

This chapter offers a new method for advancing an organization toward its competitive goals. Cycle time is a simple but powerful measurement. The learning curve is an arithmetic projection that most calculators and desktop computers can easily plot. From there it is relatively easy to figure out proficiency rates and the proficiency curve. These new metrics for speed are fundamental to changing the focus from training events to the overall process by which workers become proficient. Successful leaders will use them to modify decisions, add resources, and check regularly for improvement. They will use these concepts as they were intended, as simple tools grounded in good common business sense. Keep them that way and the result will quickly move the people of your organization forward to proficiency.

Music You Can See:
The Rhythm from Companies
that Put It All Together

Common to these organizations is a beat, a source of energy, a rhythm. These organizations seem to have discovered the difference between a single random event and a pattern of strategic activities that creates a percussive rhythm of continuous, targeted actions to promote faster learning.

When I began the research for this book in 1994, I was thoroughly convinced that learning and workforce proficiency were the essence of productive activity and overall competitiveness. Today, after working with more than one third of the *Fortune 50* companies and numerous midsized and small organizations, I am more certain than ever that this is true. I am equally certain, however, that there is no one recipe for success that is common among leading organizations. Early on, this created a serious dilemma for my research because I was truly seeking the validation of a "best practice," a standard process adhered to by companies that excelled at developing their people and competing in the marketplace.

"There is no single critical act, no step-by-step process, no matchless system for sharing information, and no formula common to organizations that learn fast." This is what I scratched on the top of my notepad during a long flight from New York to Denver. I was returning from a week-long trip that included successful meetings with leaders at IBM and Arrow Electronics. At the time (as they are today), both companies were market leaders on a number of fronts, and both organizations had a distinct vision and strategy for the development of their workers.

At IBM, which has one of the world's largest workforces, Lou Gerstner was successfully rebuilding a company that could compete with nimble Silicon Valley competitors. Through a form of a "grass-roots revival," the agents of change within IBM worked with a new mantra: "Rules for radicals." These leaders were given license to work on the edge—to find creative methods to bring "network-centric computing" to life and to build a workforce that could rapidly produce and support competitive products and services.[1] Tom Bouchard, the top human resources officer and a direct report to Gerstner, brought in Janet McAllister, a respected and seasoned operations "radical," to reinvigorate IBM's learning process. McAllister became their leader of Global Learning and started what has become a remarkable turnaround in the way people at IBM learn. True to the strategy of "network-centric computing," McAllister, who now leads a successful Bay Area Internet company, researched at length the way IBM employees prefer to learn and then built self-paced, technology-driven systems to deliver learning instantly via the Web nearly anywhere on earth. By applying knowledge of employee-learning preferences to new technology-based delivery, IBM has helped learners to accept fast new ways to learn and practice. Learning speed has increased dramatically, with employees, especially new employees, able to learn at speeds only "radicals" could imagine.[2]

My second visit that week was to a very different place, Arrow Electronics, a company that continues to hold a remarkable lead in the global distribution of electronic components. This multibillion-dollar enterprise is small in comparison to IBM but larger than life when it comes to the know-how of its workforce. Stephen Kaufman, the venerable CEO, has a strategy at the opposite pole from that of IBM. He believes in a "high-touch," low-tech strategy for learning that technologists would call old-fashioned: his organization invests in lengthy classroom courses and extensive coaching time with subject matter experts. The process at Arrow Electronics is successful because of a relentless concentration on the learner who is attempting to reach proficiency. Very little is left to chance in the learning process as coaches and mentors assist learners from the classroom to the workspace. Arrow Electronics is also expert at using otherwise wasted time to its advantage. For example, at its annual sales conference, which in most companies is mostly recognition and hoopla, they design simulations and practice sessions to help salespeople rapidly come up to speed on the new product offerings and value propositions. When they leave the three-day conference, members of the sales force are already proficient with the new products. Kaufman considers himself and his leadership team the teachers and the ultimate role models for learning. In this case, "old-fashioned" may actually be "fashionable," in that Arrow may have one of the best-developed, most proficient management teams in the industry. The learning speed and operational proficiency at Arrow are proof that using technology, the Web, and self-paced learning is not the only successful approach to increasing organizational learning speed.[3]

The stark contrast between IBM's bias for technology and Arrow Electronics' traditional approach should be noted. Both companies are champions in the race to organizational proficiency, yet they use radically different methods to get their organization ready to compete. The common denominator is that both companies truly understand the need for reaching the proficiency threshold quickly and have found creative ways to achieve this target that are consistent with their successful cultures.

Breakaway

Rhythm and the Rules

The rules for delivering value fast that were highlighted in the previous three chapters govern the sequence and direction of an enterprise's plan to begin to achieve rapid rates to proficiency. Momentum that will sustain and drive the improvements will come from the energy and creativity applied to the rules. There are organizations today that have reduced the cycle time to proficiency for a specific skill by as much as 80 percent. Common to these organizations is a beat, a source of energy, a rhythm. These organizations seem to have discovered the difference between a single random event and a pattern of strategic activities that creates a percussive rhythm of continuous, targeted actions to promote faster learning. When witnessing one of these organizations in action, one finds a relentless source of personal and operational energy directed at consuming new knowledge, learning, and performing.

This source of energy, this rhythm, is often strikingly different from one company to the next, but a similar pattern of traits, ideas, and behaviors is always present and gives definition to the rhythm. To my mind, six features make up this pattern in organizations that learn fast. The rhythm always begins with the first feature, a core belief that proficient workers represent a significant business advantage. The remaining five features are played out differently, highlighting many unique approaches toward creating a breakaway. I call these six features *priority, impatience, learners as consumers, simplicity, technology,* and *candor.*

108

Workforce Proficiency as Organizational Priority

This feature is the common denominator among companies that have separated themselves from the competition
with a proficient workforce. Learning in these companies
is a clear priority and is given the same importance as
other key strategic investments. Training efforts in organizations that dance to this beat are in lockstep with immediate business needs and are not managed as isolated
activities or events to schedule during downtime. Most, if
not all, of these organizations use business metrics to
measure their progress. The Balanced Scorecard, discussed in Chapter 3, is becoming an increasingly popular
tool to integrate learning with an organization's strategic
goals, along with measures such as financial performance, customer satisfaction efforts, and internal cost management.[4]

Speed Provokes Impatience with Wasted Activity

People in these organizations want to break away from
the pack, and nothing frustrates them more than a slow,
bureaucratic system for training. Their central belief is
that they can learn faster, and that belief promotes actions
that make faster learning possible. Workers talk of knowledge and learning in the context of customers, market
share, and profit. "New knowledge and improved performance" is their mantra, and they thrive on learning,
anytime and anywhere. They aren't afraid of trial-and-
error learning; rather, they relish it—the faster, the better.
In this environment, facilitators and instructors are
focused on performance and results. Their ultimate goal is
developing skilled and proficient employees, not planning

People in these organizations want to break away from the pack, and nothing frustrates them more than a slow, bureaucratic system for training. Their central belief is that they can learn faster, and that belief promotes actions that make faster learning possible.

training events or scheduling activities. As Patricia Asp, vice president of ServiceMaster, put it, "I lay awake at night and worry that my competitor is rapidly developing worker know-how while we are massaging our calendars to find a time to decide what to do next. I believe there is direct correlation between our ability to learn faster and our impatience for the status quo."[5]

Seeing the Employee as a Consumer of Learning

Jinny Goldstein, former president and CEO of PBS The Business Channel, has a vision and a passion for what she dubs "the learner-centered environment. She also has the character and the presence to command the attention of the toughest audiences. When she describes the future in terms of the creating an environment specifically to meet the needs of different learners, people listen. Goldstein envisions a virtual "learning-neural system" that surrounds a worker with options for content, delivery choice, and reinforcement that erases the line between work and learning.[6]

Organizations that have achieved the rhythm of speed to proficiency view employees as the consumers of all learning investments. This idea reflects a crucial shift in perspective that enables enormous opportunity for faster learning. Today's employees browse the Web, absorb the news, and converse with customers, internalizing a vivid picture of the changes taking place around them. Even when away from work, they continue to consume information—learning has become second nature to them. This strategy understands that when the learning methods within the workplace are out of sync with those in the world outside the corporate walls, learning becomes contrived and unnatural and, ultimately, slows to a crawl. Fast-learning organizations take advantage of the abundance of information and technology available outside the workplace; they reap the reward of faster learning by synchronizing with the daily, natural learning of their workforce.

Decision makers in fast-learning organizations also understand that workers must want to learn before there is any chance of application. Therefore, they attempt to identify the individual learning needs and preferences of workers and to fashion learning activities that can quickly translate into knowledge applied on the job.

The Link between Simplicity and Speed

Making the connection between simplicity and speed is a common attribute among companies striving to reach proficiency faster. Organizations that are making the learning process simpler in order to speed up knowledge acquisition do not break a complex system into its component parts.[7] Instead, they start with a simple system and resist the urge to create a stable, engineered system for learning. Simple also comes in smaller pieces and modules. Organizations in today's competitive economy can't afford to put their employees through lengthy training sessions or wait for them to complete a full course before they are able to bring new skills and knowledge to their jobs. Shorter learning modules allow workers to achieve a specific learning objective quickly and to begin using new knowledge immediately. "The smallest teachable unit" is the goal for Patrick Hernandez, vice president of New Century Energies, a large utility provider in the Rocky Mountains. "We can design, develop, and teach a one-hour module in the time it takes to design a one-day course." Hernandez helped lead the merger between Public Service of Colorado and a large utility provider in northern Texas. "The only way to bring two management cultures together was to keep the learning process as simple and flexible as possible."[8]

Flexibility is a sibling of simplicity. A fixed method for delivery and reinforcement begs for complexity in design and implementation. Flexibility requires forethought and a bias toward the less complicated. As one teacher put it, "The new facilitator guide must help me stand in front of a class, talk to a video recorder, shrink the key contents into a reinforcing voice mail message, and announce the availability of all three on our Web page." Finally, the companies that get full return from their simple approach have a bias toward authenticity and try to dispel the ambiguity that arises from overly complex instructional design and methods. The more rigid, inflexible, and contrived the materials, the more difficult they are to explain, the greater the possibility for inconsistencies to emerge, and the more likely that the reasons for learning will be obscured.

Technology: Innovating to Learn

My eleven-year-old son and his friend recently found a way to use SEGA and Nintendo controllers interchangeably. The process wasn't pretty, but it allowed them to get more players in the video game without buying additional controllers. Although I am certain that the manufacturers would be concerned about this, I am also certain that the manufacturers don't view technology like my son does. He and his friends use a new word, *technovate*, to describe their experiments, which use technology as a commodity and their minds as the ever-increasing source of innovative ideas.

Payoff from advances in technology will come when we use it in ways never before imagined. When used intelligently, today's information technology (sometimes called IT) can dramatically reduce the cycle time to proficiency, rapidly advancing an organization. Specifically, improvements in desktop multimedia and Internet/Intranet applications promise innovative applications in learning. This powerful new class of information technology offers extraordinary strategic advantage to those who use it creatively. As precisely as a surgeon's scalpel, today's technology enables an organization to pair an individual with the right content at the right time. For the first time in history, we have virtually eliminated the barriers of time and space for linking the worker with new information.

Unfortunately, many companies are using this new capacity merely to automate methods already used in conventional training. Making information continuously available to workers through innovations in technology takes courage from leaders. As nervous as access to the Internet makes many decision makers, it is Internet browsing that transforms a worker from someone who waits for formal training into a proactive, curious learner. Now that information is available in various forms of multimedia, the responsibility for learning and ultimately performing can be placed where it belongs—with the worker.

This advantage alone should persuade cautious decision makers of the advantages of adopting a serious information technology delivery strategy. An enterprise today is defined by its use of information. *Connectivity*, the new buzzword, is the key to leveraging today's technology. Information and the mechanisms for delivering it link people together. Access to this information will facilitate a person's ability to learn and act quickly. From interactive kiosks arranged to accommodate the manufacturing flow of a factory to handheld devices for airplane mechanics working in tight spaces, the technology that allows us to quickly find or receive information is now ubiquitous. In an environment where the opportunity for development comes in transient spurts, technology affords workers the means to reach proficiency despite the physical con-straints of the operation. The ability to log into a learning session whenever time is available and in a readily acces-sible environment is a boon to all the workers whose situ-ation previously made it difficult to participate in train-ing. Perhaps the most powerful lever of anytime-anyplace learning is the fact that it allows a business to tie the learning process directly to the value proposition. If the initial learning is juxtaposed with the accumulation of experience in the workplace, then workers can instantly integrate a short technology-based session with their per-formance and immediately practice using the newly acquired knowledge and information.

Candor: Seeing Things as They Really Are

"If we can't ask the tough questions and take on the obstacles that are keeping our people from learning fast, then how can we expect our business to improve and grow?" asks Sam Reese, vice president and business development guru of Kinko's.[9] He believes that honesty and candor about training that isn't working is the ulti-mate catalyst toward learning faster.

Organizations that have
achieved the rhythm of
speed to proficiency view
employees as the consumers
of all learning investments.

Rarely are all the obstacles removed before we move ahead, but the people within fast-learning companies courageously ask tough questions about why things aren't working, and the obstacles to learning are the first to be scrutinized. Workers challenge the assumptions about learning that slow them down, and they would rather expose them than ignore them. Being unafraid to see things as they really are allows organizations to explore new and better ways to reach proficiency. They may err toward the practical, yet their businesses can more quickly and thoroughly implement new technology and distance-based instruction than can companies chasing the latest fad. Few of these companies have a "director of training"; when asked who is in charge of training, the finger is usually pointed toward the front office. Their leaders teach and their teachers lead, and they aren't particularly concerned about which role they are playing—as long as the learners are tapping their feet to the rhythm of proficiency—if they aren't, someone says so.

The Operational Advantages of the Rhythm

In all of the fast-learning companies I examined, these six features combine so that each company seems to "dance to a different beat." However, all the companies that champion the message of this book have found a passionate, high-speed *rhythm* for reaching proficiency faster.

Table 6.1 compares how these six factors associated with faster cycle time to proficiency work in a sample of fast-learning organizations. The distribution of marks in the table columns illustrates how organizations that learn quickly create their own individual rhythm, not drawing

Six Ingredients for Speed to Proficiency

	Priority	Impatience	Learners as Consumers	Simplicity	Technology	Candor
Starbucks Retail (Partner) Development	●	●	●	●		
Hewlett-Packard Product Information and Sales	●	●			●	●
Platinum Technologies Global Sales	●	●	●		●	
U.S. Army National Training Center Leadership Development	●		●		●	●
Sun Microsystems C++ and Java Programmer Development	●			●	●	
Kinko's Supervisor and Management Training	●		●		●	
PBS The Business Channel Overall Business Strategy	●		●	●	●	
IBM Global Learning Strategy	●		●		●	
ServiceMaster Technical Skill Development Leadership Development	●			●		
New Century Energies Management Development	●	●	●	●		●
Arrow Electronics Orientation and Global Sales	●	●	●			●

Table 6.1

on any prescribed notions of the mix or degree of what's important, but finding and applying their own indisputable recipe for success.

Ultimately, creating a rhythm for speed to proficiency produces significant operational advantages. An organization must build the capacity to serve the customer more quickly and effectively than the competition. The rhythm, once created, stimulates a number of competitive advantages that are extraordinarily difficult for the competition to duplicate.

Operational Agility

Lack of know-how is one of the most constricting bottlenecks in the delivery of service. A bottleneck, created when the capacity of any resource is less than the demand placed upon it, constrains an operation's ability to produce. In the industrial-based economy, machine tools, equipment, and transportation were the resources typically responsible for bottlenecks. Today, the resource that is most likely to fail to meet the demands upon it is the nonproficient worker—the worker who doesn't have the necessary skills to perform. Manufacturers increase capacity by managing the bottlenecks. Saving an hour by unclogging the bottleneck not only adds an extra hour to the entire process that follows but also recovers lost profit for the entire system. By returning an hour to a service process that is constrained, you can generate a huge amount of additional capacity. A workforce that can obtain new skills faster than that of the competition can give an organization the additional capacity needed to take the marketplace by storm.

There is also an enormous personal benefit. At a certain point, people exceed their ability to absorb more change—the pace of change has simply overtaken their ability to integrate new processes or systems. This is when people become ill or experience emotional burnout, and eventually signs of dysfunction can become evident throughout the organization. Having the skills to perform at an acceptable level enables individual workers to accept and make the transition to the next wave of change. Organizations that have a critical mass of workers who possess the know-how to handle variable requests from customers, who can work around the multiple nuances within most delivery processes, and who can absorb and tackle the next set of changes thrown at them will sustain a long-term competitive advantage.

Real and Sustained Quality Improvements

The single greatest obstacle to improving quality systematically is the glacial pace at which organizations acquire the necessary skills for improvement. Take, for example, programs for training staff in the tools and techniques of total quality management (TQM). Many organizations have multiyear training programs on TQM, with few workers getting past the introduction stage of learning. Imagine the advantage to a company whose workers are not only familiar with but are using these skills while their competition still struggles to introduce them. This advantage highlights the biggest contrast between efforts to reach proficiency faster and the typical training approach. Decision makers who understand the full leverage of proficient workers armed with quality improvement tools and techniques will give priority to getting the frontline product and service workers to proficiency first. In contrast, the typical training approach is to put managers into classes first so that they can understand and monitor the TQM effort as it slowly unfolds. The competitive contrast between these two methods is huge.

Workers armed with know-how produce improved product and service quality without fail. The advantage to quickly having a cadre of workers who can take very good care of the customer or provide defect-free products is thus enormous. And the alternative can be fatal. Organizations with slow and clumsy methods of reaching proficiency fall continually farther behind a competitor with a service-capable workforce. While the slower competitor is searching for new learning methods, the one with a proficient workforce is improving and refining an already advantageous system. The gap may become so large that catching up is impossible.

Employee Retention

The nation's current unemployment rate—around 4 percent—remains at a twenty-five-year low. The movement of knowledgeable workers from one company to the next is taking place at a furious pace. Organizations that can retain proficient workers will have a significant advantage for two reasons. First, proficient workers by definition provide value to customers, contribute to the development of the next new product or service, and anticipate and solve problems—they know how to work with and around the operating system. Second, these proficient workers will not end up serving customers for another company. The loss of a proficient, productive worker in today's economy is a costly event. Not only is there a loss

Organizations that are

making the learning process

simpler in order to speed up

knowledge acquisition do not

break a complex system into

its component parts. Instead,

they start with a simple

system and resist the urge to

create a stable, engineered

system for learning.

of the time and money invested to develop the worker to proficiency, but an equivalent investment will be needed to develop a new worker to an equivalent level.

According to a recent study by the U.S. Department of Labor, the fastest growing occupations and those most vulnerable to turnover include database administrators, computer scientists and engineers, and personal and home care aides. The internal costs to replace one of those workers in their first year could be as high as one year's salary. For those who have more than one year of experience, these costs skyrocket.

Organizations that have a system for getting employees to proficiency faster have a far greater chance of retaining them. Proficient workers contribute and add value to the process of which they are a part. Being able to make a contribution has a direct impact on morale, which in turn correlates with longevity in the organization. Those who can attain proficiency faster will also be promoted more quickly, gain the respect of their peers, earn a sense of accomplishment through serving customers well, and thus will be less likely to leave.

Finding good people may be one of the biggest challenges companies face as we begin the third millennium. Focusing on recruiting young workers won't solve most companies' hiring problems over the long term because Generation X is significantly smaller than the generation of baby boomers that preceded it. In addition, organizations can't simply address the problem by raising wages. With inflation hovering around 3 percent, a thirty-year low, they must contain costs and prices to stay competitive. In today's economy and for the foreseeable future, organizations must create and retain proficient and creative workers.

Getting workers to proficiency fast and enabling them to contribute and develop further is the best retention strategy available. Organizations that can attract and retain workers will not only be able to intimidate their high-turnover competition, but they will also benefit by attracting their competition's best people.

The Leadership Agenda: Taking People from Where They Are To Where They Need to Be—Fast

This new agenda will move

the center of gravity of an

organization toward the rapid

development of its people.

The leadership agenda is changing once again. The focus of the past five years was on restructuring costs, preparing for Y2K, and developing strategies for growth. Today, growth is still the overarching agenda topic, but one of the biggest problems facing leaders with aggressive growth targets is how to develop their organization's social fabric so that it can learn at breakneck speed. My recent discussions with business leaders indicate that "the organization" has moved back onto the center stage of the leadership agenda. Leaders, specifically CEOs, are beginning to take more seriously some of the training and development concepts that they recently only nominally supported.

This shift is partly a logical follow-through for companies that have completed necessary cost restructuring and infrastructure development for e-commerce. Leaders must now look to revenue growth for the next leap in performance, and this growth can only come from customers. To a large extent, the renewed emphasis on the organization coincides with a movement to reintroduce the employees of the enterprise with its customers. The fizzle of the dot-com notion that eyeballs can replace revenue as the primary driver of value only reinforces the agenda of preparing the organization's people to propel growth. Leaders seeking to capture differentiated growth in revenue through the proficiency of their "organization" are establishing a new agenda. This new agenda has four principal themes:

- Creating an obsession for preparing the workforce to compete and deliver value
- Embracing and leading the Net Generation

- Attracting and retaining the free-agent worker
- Bringing innovation to the development of people

Creating the Obsession

The headquarters of the ServiceMaster Corporation in Downers Grove, Illinois, would surprise most people. Instead of a towering glass-and-brass facility with an imposing lobby—what you might expect for a $5 billion corporation—it is a renovated single-level building with an open foyer. Along with an expansive granite wall on which ServiceMaster's core values are etched, the lobby is dominated by a convex-shaped wall of white-framed windows enclosing the company's showpiece—a classroom. This classroom is more than a functional space where many hours of learning have occurred; it is a physical metaphor for what the leaders and people of ServiceMaster believe: their *business* is developing people.

Every few weeks, you will find chairman Bill Pollard or CEO Carlos Cantu teaching in that classroom. On another day, you will find them both learning—from faculty of the Harvard Business School, for example, or from customers who are invited to talk about their products and service requirements, or from their own employees and franchise owners.

The fundamental reason for the enormous growth and success of ServiceMaster is its unparalleled drive to develop people. Today this company, possibly better known for its market-leading consumer businesses such as TruGreen, ChemLawn, Terminix, Merry Maids, and American Home Shield, is the world's leading service company, achieving twenty-six consecutive years of growth in revenues and profits. It employs more than 200,000 workers and serves more than 6 million customers in thirty-one countries.

Because of Pollard's and Cantu's obsession, ServiceMaster continually builds value by developing smart, professional workers and placing them in front of customers. Their success is not based on taking up some recent training fad or using a new technology, but on an unwavering commitment to make employee development their top priority. Bill Pollard listens, learns, and teaches every day. His actions set the leadership expectations at ServiceMaster. At the beginning of a teaching session, for example, he asks his audience: "Am I prepared to serve as I lead, to listen as I promote, to learn as I teach, to commit as I expect others to follow, to build on the ordinary as I expect the extraordinary, and to develop people as I seek to grow profits?"

What most distinguishes leaders who can continuously spark organizations to succeed and prosper from those who cannot is their fierce commitment to learn, to teach, and to develop people. A corporate leader's thirst for listening, learning, and applying new knowledge produces a cascading effect throughout the organization. Through their own actions and behaviors, such leaders create a dynamic culture of knowledge sharing and teaching.

One sales employee of Buckman Laboratories, a leading chemical company located in Memphis, described his company's obsession for learning. "Discovering new information and sharing it with everybody is as popular and career advancing here as a good golf game was at my previous employer. Bob [Buckman] defines our culture.

His leadership in the area of learning and knowledge management influences all of us, and because of his tenacity in building 'The Knowledge Network,' we are believers and practitioners."[1] Long a leading light in the knowledge management movement, Bob Buckman now has a system at Buckman Laboratories that brings associates in over eighty countries together to share knowledge in solving customer problems. Leaders like Buckman forge a new way of doing business and establish the benchmark through their own learning activity.

Bob Galvin, Sr., of Motorola is another leader with a passion for learning and teaching. He made Motorola a global leader in the production of high-quality electronic products at a time when Japan was eating nearly every other American manufacturer for lunch. Today, in his senior years, he continues to be obsessed with helping Motorola employees learn and compete. I was working at US West when I had the opportunity to hear Galvin, then chairman of Motorola, explain the methods Motorola used to reach a world-class position. At the time, US West was in the process of establishing a leadership council to address business issues concerning learning and training, and our chairman, Richard McCormick, invited Galvin to speak to the leadership team. The obsession and passion we observed in the venerable, confident Galvin changed the way many of us viewed our priorities and our people.

He began his address by discussing the way Motorola views their learners, their training, and the cost of developing people. "Training at Motorola has never cost us any money because the cost of *not* training far outweighs any cost associated with it. If we train a person on SPC [statistical process control] in the first quarter and it costs $500, we know that person will be at least $500 more productive in the second [quarter]. We also know that our current cost [because] of poor quality is far greater than any cost associated with training. This thinking is axiomatic for us, and some may say I am presumptuous about the results. If you don't believe that your investment will pay off in this way, it won't. I have a few doubters. I tell them to look at my numbers—and I don't hear from them again."[2]

Galvin's unabashed belief in employee development and learning inspired all of us who listened to this sage business leader. Because of his intense desire to create a workforce that could compete with that of any engineering and manufacturing company around the globe, his team responded accordingly and the company achieved world-class status.

An obsession for developing proficiency means also making it a top priority. Phil Condit, the accomplished leader of the Boeing Company, found time to complete his doctorate in engineering while tackling the largest aerospace merger in history. Through his personal example, he demonstrated to his organization the belief that knowledge and proficiency will take Boeing into the third millennium as the leader not only in commercial aerospace but in engineering, manufacturing, and assembly knowledge as well. This has long been his guiding philosophy, and Boeing continues to attract and develop the best engineering and assembly talent on the planet.

Breakaway

Leading the Net Generation

Expertise requires education, and much of what we have
known as education and employee development is changing before our eyes. The way it is funded, designed, managed, and delivered will change more in the next few
years than it has in the past century. The first evidence of
this change is the dramatic acceleration of technology,
especially the growth of the Internet as a tool for learning.
Today's technology and the inherent ubiquity of the
Internet have cut down the traditional barriers of time,
space, and cost. Workshops, seminars, customized training events, and competitive information previously available only to those companies with abundant resources are
now available to anyone with Internet access. The eco-
nomics of learning are changing fast, and small, nimble
companies can now obtain new information and reach
proficiency within an affordable cost model. The emer-
gence of online education and information is not only a
matter of technological change, but also of access.
Anytime-anywhere access to information, content, and
methodology will enable a worker to develop a new orientation to time and space as it relates to their learning
and development. Reaching proficiency will become a
continuous process that replaces one-time training events.

But technology is not the only movement behind the
recent advances in learning. The people that work with
that technology, especially young people, are key. For the
"Net generation," a group of young adults so comfortable
with technology that they think it is all part of the original
plan, life and learning without a technology twist is simply unacceptable.[3] Armed with the will to learn and an

intimate knowledge of current technology, they will be a formidable force, and a positive one, for organizations that foster a youthful culture. These "kids," some 80 million strong in the United States alone, are just now entering the job market and becoming employed. Combined with an already digitally literate X-generation, they will soon represent the majority of workers in the service and technology sectors of our country. If you have met a group of these young adults as students in a traditional classroom, you know firsthand that a change in our traditional method of learning is under way. The leverage of technology as a learning tool today is only constrained by those who resist it. Technology, specifically the Internet, will continue to force changes in the way people learn. Even for those in a "wait and see" mode, the force coming from the Net generation will soon be too great to ignore.

Attracting the Free-Agent Worker

If you don't think that technology and youth will change the way we work and learn, then pay close attention to the incumbent worker who is attempting to learn and perform in today's corporations. First of all, the "free-agent movement" is real, and employees who see themselves as free agents will only increase in numbers. This movement gives leaders pause; they wonder if they are developing people for their competition rather than for themselves and, at the same time, they worry about how they will ever fill their current staffing needs. Companies with a less-than-rapid pace for learning stand to lose a significant amount of their investment whenever proficient workers leave for another company just as they reach the threshold level of performance.

Compound the free-agent movement with the dramatic changes in the demographics of today's workforce, and you see that the fundamental reshaping of the current system for training is inevitable. Key decision makers need to work under the assumption that the average new employee will be critically unprepared to serve the customer, at least initially, and may even need basic skills in reading and writing.

The demographics of the workforce that will replace the baby-boomer generation presents business with a very different set of issues. Twenty-five million new workers will join the workforce in the first decade of the twenty-first century alone,[4] and only a small percentage of these new workers will fit the previous profile of a worker. For example, one in five of the new workers will be immigrants, many non-English speaking. A National Association of Manufacturers survey of 4,000 members concluded that, "60 percent of new jobs will require more than a high school education. However, 70 percent of new entrants into the workforce will have less than a high school degree."[5] Worker-starved companies will adopt sick-child leave, part-time and at-home work policies, on-site day care, and numerous language literacy programs. Information will need to be presented in non-classroom formats and available day or night. Clearly, the enormous skill gap created by dramatic demographic changes in the national workforce will change the way we approach work and learning—forever.

Innovation and the Development of People

Innovation has long been the hallmark of market-leading companies. Invention and ingenuity in product development, packaging, marketing, and technology have created significant opportunity and growth for companies that can "out-innovate" their competition. As important as product innovation and improvement have been to the success of a business in the past, however, the most important innovation today is in the development of people. For all the advances we have realized in manufacturing technology, telecommunications, and computing, little has changed about the learning process in corporations.

Hal Rosenbluth, the innovative CEO of Rosenbluth Travel, has always been ahead of his time. He captures many of his creative "people development" ideas in his popular book, *The Customer Comes Second: And Other Secrets of Exceptional Service*. Rosenbluth Travel has been written about and admired as a global industry leader, noted not for its sophisticated reservation and scheduling system or its robust Web site but for its unmatched creativity in developing people—and its resulting growth and profits. Rosenbluth believes that a prepared, proficient work force is the antecedent to happy customers, and in fact his concentrated energy and creativity in development issues like learning methods, compensation, and performance reviews have produced great financials. Learning at Rosenbluth Travel is fun, continuous, and radically different than traditional corporate instruction. Many of the training staff at this travel company have theater or arts backgrounds and deep experience in the daily work of the agency, and they use creative ideas to make

135

learning engaging. The company has established a "transitional learning center" to help new hires ease into the mainstream of the business. The learning process at Rosenbluth Travel has been so successful that there is a waiting list for people who want to be a part of this ingenious process—not a waiting list for employees of Rosenbluth Travel, but for their customers.

Injecting innovation and energy into the learning process can awaken the sleepiest of organizations. A purposeful, innovative act from a leader can spark a learning revolution and transform an organization struggling with change. Jerry Johnson is the senior vice president of operations for Safeguard Scientifics, a hugely successful firm that has enabled companies like Novell, Cambridge Technology Partners, and the Internet Capital Group (ICG) to grow successfully, leading ultimately to successful Initial Public Offerings. Prior to joining Safeguard Scientifics, Johnson ran one of the largest field forces in the telecommunications industry. More than 30,000 employees in fourteen states worked in his operation. In 1994, Johnson was responsible for a major reengineering effort that had fallen seriously behind schedule and was faltering. The newly designed processes were not producing sufficiently to meet customer demand, the computer system upgrades were months behind schedule, and the confidence of the workers was declining rapidly. When Johnson asked his senior management team to diagnose the problem, it was clear they were out of touch with the workers who were desperately trying to meet commitments and serve customers. Most managers were attempting to solve problems from a knowledge base that was obsolete and in many cases actually ran counter to the reengineering effort. A wacky, innovative learning idea changed all that. Johnson, who had also been a teacher and educator, decided that the members of his leadership team needed to become students and relearn how to run the business—from the workers who were doing it.

In a letter to his leadership team, Johnson initiated a process that would ultimately transform his team, the workers, and customer service. Johnson's letter called for the leadership team to undertake what might be called a "mission of discovery" about the company to allow them to "rediscover and learn from the collective knowledge of your employees by joining your fellow leaders in studentship. The method will require courage to admit the unknown, hard work to learn again, and willingness to allow employees to guide your studies and impart their knowledge to you. The result will place you in a position of leadership, not of weakness, and build a relationship with employees, a relationship we need to move this organization forward. It is time for us to get back in touch with the core of this business and lead it forward."[6]

Johnson designated a two-week period for this "study mission" and instructed his executives and managers to clear their calendars. He told his group that they would be traveling by bus to selected operational sites and "listening and learning from our employees." To ensure that the visits to the company sites would "get below the typical cosmetic surface of prepared presentation and discussion," Johnson kept the itinerary of the journey a secret. He explained that the group would be "traveling to places rarely seen and talking to employees who may have strong opinions. Treasure is in the unknown and uncomfortable."

In his letter, Johnson laid out the ground rules for his team: "I require five behaviors from each of you:

- Admit to not knowing—'I recognize there is a lot I don't know'
- Be a buddy—learn to rely on each other
- Use discipline—adhere to agreed-upon guidelines and norms
- Exercise 'studentship'—become a student and a teacher
- Be willing to change—act upon new learning"

He continued: "A bias to learn requires genuinely seeking out information, ideas, and feedback that may run counter to our current assumptions. If our current leadership culture is one of always having the information and answers, we will never change fast enough to survive. Courage to listen and admit the unknown is our first step in becoming the leaders needed to run this organization. Instead of being perceived as weak, we will begin to build respect and rapport with our workers.

"Learning to depend on others and to be reliable and trustworthy is an integral part of this mission. One cannot survive the trip without the assistance of a 'buddy,' just as a business cannot survive without an authentic relationship between the management team and the employees. Building this relationship starts with your own team. As in the real world, not all information is given to you. Seeking to know and understand is the behavior that will open our currently closed minds. For example, you may know where the morning meeting place is, and your buddy may know the time. A responsible buddy checks to make certain his or her partner is on the bus when departing, has the study guide for each visit, and meets all conduct guidelines. Additionally, your buddy will become a confidant and counselor for the exhausting days of our discovery. Imagine our management team supporting each other in this way every day. Becoming a veritable buddy starts to break down the facade of 'knowledge is power.' In this case, knowledge is potent only if combined with your partner's information. This study mission will expose the impact of combining the collective wisdom of employees with the insight of the management team, our system for the future."

Johnson wanted his study group to develop an agreed-upon strict set of behavioral norms—conduct necessary to sustain congeniality and good will while they spent nearly sixteen hours a day together—and he proposed fines for anyone who violated those norms. "The amount of money is not the central idea behind the fine but rather the commitment made to each other and personal pride to uphold the commitment." His buddy system was designed to strengthen the reliability of each individual. "Finding someone to rely on and to be reliable to accelerates learning about yourself and your buddy. Without a reliable buddy, adhering to all the behavioral agreements is nearly impossible."

Johnson concluded his letter with these words: "Finally, the commitment to act and change following the study mission must be resolute and made before our first lesson. If you have any doubt that this mission will help us learn and run this organization better, let me know now. After our employees have exposed their hearts and minds to us, we must act upon their teaching and make the necessary changes. If we don't, never again will they believe management to be genuine or trustworthy. The knowledge we will gain during this study mission is powerful enough to transform any company, business, or organization. I trust you all will join me in this important effort."

Johnson's invitation must have been perceived as bizarre. Most of these executives usually traveled on a corporate jet, certainly not a bus. All had climbed the corporate ladder as experts in their respective fields. Hopping on a bus to learn from the rank and file was probably not an idea they had encountered before. As skeptical as these executives may have been before the trip, however, they are believers today. For many, not only did the trip transform their leadership approach and overall knowledge, but it also changed their lives. They experienced the richness of leadership as learners and found hundreds of new sources of information to make better decisions. And as for speed to proficiency, nothing compares to the real-time experience of this kind of mission.

I believe that the new agenda in this book will move the center of gravity of an organization toward the rapid development of its people. Successful leaders will be those who can organize and accelerate this development, not purely for the benevolent reasons of life-long learning, but for the hard-line competitiveness of the firm. As the leadership agenda continues to develop, the natural question is whether the focus is the right one. From my examination, the new agenda is properly directed, not because great minds created it, but because survival will demand it. Remember, those that lead their organizations to break away from the competition will enjoy market share and revenue growth never before imaginable. But the breakaway will absolutely require a proficient work force that can deliver on its promises to customers.

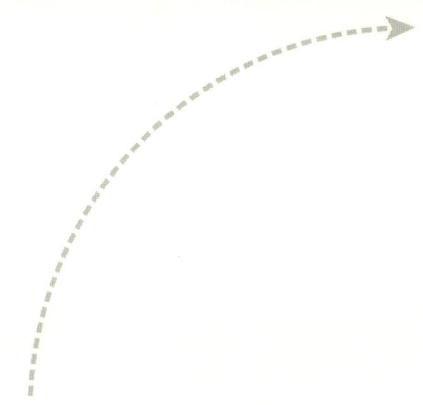

Afterword

True leaders must take

people from where they are

today to where they need to

be tomorrow, and get them

there fast.

M y friend and colleague Paul sat saddle-style with his forearms resting lazily over the back of his chair and watched the video of our new executive summarizing the current condition of our company. Slowly Paul lowered his head and rested it on his arms. I watched as he and others digested and pondered the message.

"The marketplace is changing and driving us to be more competitive," our executive began. "New competitors are targeting our customers and could gain significant market share in a very short period of time. We are too burdened with labor, too slow in our process improvements, and need contemporary skills to compete effectively. Our customers demand this from us, and they are the reason we must change and change fast.

"Our new strategy calls for streamlining our processes. The game has changed, and we, the leaders of this company, choose to play and protect our market share. We must start to move faster, increase productivity, and delight the customers with outstanding service. If you want to be a part of this new team, get on board with this way of thinking and make the necessary changes immediately."

Paul looked at me with an ashen face, clearly stunned by the message. Just the week before we had celebrated his twenty-fifth year of service at the company. Times were good, and one could count on being rewarded for hard work and commitment.

Now the rules and the game had changed—seemingly overnight. But these changes had not really occurred that quickly. We had been so busy running the business, so satisfied with the status quo, that the pace of change surrounding our business went unnoticed. We were caught off guard and completely unprepared for what had now become an operational emergency.

Only a month later, after a painful restructuring effort, Paul and I assessed the wreckage of the organization. He and many others had made the decision to take a buy-out and retire early. I listened to him articulate his reasons for leaving a place where he had spent half his life. Here was a man who had survived two tours in Vietnam, a painful divorce, and a near-fatal car crash, but he couldn't make it any longer in his job. He rationalized his decision with complaints about his lack of skill in a new economy and an overall lack of energy to deal with constant change.

I watched Paul walk out of the factory that day, his coat slung over one arm, metal lunch box and thermos in the other, pushing past the heavy metal doors as he had for many years, knowing that this time he was not coming back. Instead of a celebratory retirement party and a well-wishing send-off, he joined others at the local bar to ponder an uncertain future.

Many others followed in his footsteps and surrendered, leaving our organization with enormous skill gaps. Each person who left took the process and service knowledge of our company with them. Collectively we lost the neural system that allowed us to manage the daily variables in our complex business.

Soon thereafter, the company's senior leaders were summoned to attend a strategic meeting to address the critical skill deficiency at the core of the company. We spent the first hour debating the reasons for our dilemma. The excuses ranged from a general lack of strategic information about the competition to the notion that we had somehow hired the wrong people ten years ago.

All we knew was that we needed proficient people in a hurry, and we were willing to consider almost any approach to get them. Our training professionals made an impassioned presentation on the need for additional trainers and facilities and proposed an aggressive schedule to get our people up to speed. This heroic proposal required an expensive venture that would leave many of our people still unskilled for the next six months. We simply had too many people without the right skills and not enough time; clearly, it was too late for a conventional plan. Someone then proposed we hire new people with the skills we needed instead of training our remaining workforce. This somehow seemed acceptable under the circumstances: we were all under a lot of pressure to come away from this meeting with a solution.

None of us considered the consequences of this decision until after it was made. We, the leaders of a successful organization, rendered our own people disposable, perceiving them as valuable only if they were lucky enough to have just the right skills at the right time. The pressure to improve our processes quickly was so great that we ignored the most crucial process of all—enabling the people in our organization to gain the skills to make the new processes work. And somehow, we had come to the conclusion that our people were not capable of learning fast enough to catch up.

The ultimate cost of this false assumption was absolute chaos in the workplace and a dramatic decrease in our company's stock value due to exorbitant staffing costs and customer-base erosion. We seemed surprised when new workers soon exhibited skill gaps similar to those of the old workers they had replaced, as processes changed and new equipment quickly surpassed the new workers' knowledge. The ugly cycle of dumping those with obsolete skills continued until we finally realized the key to survival and growth was in retaining and developing our own people, relying on their ability to learn fast in order to deliver value to the customer.

This book is about leading with a new direction and a new focus. Our ever-changing economy offers both the motivation and the means to find new ways to reach proficiency and to perform. The true leaders who desire to create a highly competitive organization must lead people from where they are today to where they need to be tomorrow, and get them there fast. This is a much different objective than what we've seen across this country in the past decade. Those who once thought that proficient workers were readily available when you needed them— that you could acquire a new and improved version of your current workforce—are now finding not only a limited source of available people, but little loyalty for any organization among those who are available.

The great news is that the majority of people in your organization have an unlimited capacity to learn and perform at the speed of the new economy. When the decision is made to enter the race of daily change, do so with a belief that your people can rapidly become prepared to compete and win. Enter with a passion for taking the people of your organization to the future by helping them gain the knowledge and skills fast enough to realize the awesome competitive power of a breakaway.

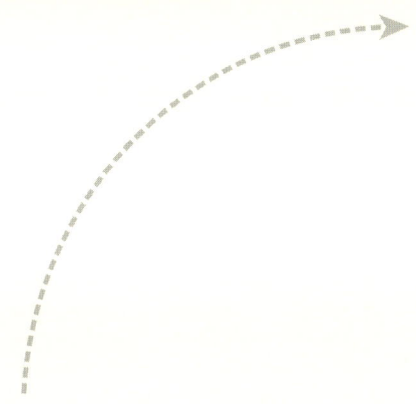

Notes

Chapter 1

1. For additional information on Home Depot's success as a high-growth retailer, see the Hardware and Home Center Industry Resource Center, an online magazine for this industry, at www.nrha.org.

2. Author interview with Wayne Brunetti, CEO of New Century Energies, February 1997. The research for this book includes 287 interviews with business leaders across the globe. The interviews were conducted between February 1993 and March 2000.

3. Robert H. Schaffer, *The Breakthrough Strategy: Using Short-Term Successes to Build the High-Performance Organization* (New York: HarperBusiness, 1988), 11–18.

Chapter 2

1. Peter F. Drucker, *Post-Capitalist Society* (New York: HarperCollins, 1989), 32–40.

2. According to *Training* Magazine's 1998 annual industry report, American companies with more than 100 employees spent a total of $56.5 billion on training.

3. In Wickliffe C. Abraham et al., *Memory Mechanisms: A Tribute to G.V. Goddard* (Hillsdale, N.J.: Lawrence Earlbaum Assoc., 1999). Goddard's insights follow the pioneering work of Hermann Ebbinghaus; see his *Memory: A Contribution to Experimental Psychology* (New York: Columbia University, 1913), translated by Henry A. Ruger and Clara E. Bussenius. For additional information about learning and memory see John R. Anderson, *Learning and Memory* (New York: John Wiley, 1994).

Chapter 3

1. Robert S. Kaplan and David P. Norton, *The Balanced Scorecard* (Boston: Harvard Business School Press, 1996), 73–76.

2. A number of sources document Dr. Deming's teaching on the internal customer-supplier relationship. One of the best is K. Ishikawa and D. Lu, *What Is Total Quality Control?* (Englewood Cliffs, N.J.:

Prentice-Hall, 1985), 73–88. The best source for a definition of the value delivery chain can be found in J. B. Quinn, *Intelligent Enterprise* (New York: The Free Press, 1992), 198–205.

Chapter 4

1. John Dewey, *How We Think* (1910; reprint New York: Prometheus Books, 1991), 52, 53. Italics added.

2. Robert M. Gagné, *Studies of Learning: 50 Years of Research* (Tallahassee, Florida: Florida State University, Learning Systems Institute, 1989), 533–537.

3. John R. Anderson, *Learning and Memory: An Integrated Approach* (New York: John Wiley, 1995), 190–209.

Chapter 5

1. C. Meyer, *Fast Cycle Time* (New York: The Free Press, 1993), 17–23.

2. H. E. Riggs, *Managing High-Technology Companies* (New York: Van Nostrand Reinhold, 1983), 95–97.

3. R.B. Chase and N. Aquilano, *Production and Operations Management: A Life Cycle Approach* (Boston: Irwin, 5th ed. 1989), 516–521.

4. James Brian Quinn, *Intelligent Enterprise* (New York: Free Press, 1992), 349–351.

5. Frederick F. Reichheld, *The Loyalty Effect: The Hidden Force Behind Growth, Profits, and Lasting Value,* (Boston: Harvard Business School Press, 1996), 122–125.

6. Howard Schultz, *Pour Your Heart Into It* (New York: Hyperion, 1997), 125, on Schultz's belief in the development of his part-time employees.

7. Author interview at Smoky Hill Starbucks in Aurora, Colorado, November 11, 1998.

8. Schultz, *Pour Your Heart Into It,* 128.

9. The estimates given on Starbucks' learning speed come from author interviews with Starbucks' employees conducted between November 11, 1997 and February 15, 2000. Partners were interviewed during their breaks at the following locations: Hyde Park in Sydney, Australia, King Street in Toronto, Canada, Clark and Madison in Chicago, Illinois, Central Avenue in Albuquerque, New Mexico, and Smokey Hill in Aurora, Colorado. These partners volunteered their experiences as learners within the Starbucks' operation. Using their information as a baseline, I calculated that creating the menu of coffee-related drinks takes nearly ten minutes in initial attempts, but that partners can dramatically reduce that time through successive practice. They estimate a 5 to 10 percent improvement with each practice session. This rapid level of improvement levels off when one can produce an espresso-based drink in less than two minutes. Fluency, however, requires this performance while under the pressure of waiting customers. This research was not sponsored or funded by the Starbucks Corporation or by its management. The interviews were on a volunteer basis by willing partners.

Chapter 6

1. "IBM's Grassroots Revival," *Fast Company* Magazine, October 1997, 183–185.

2. Author interview with Janet McAllister, IBM Vice President of Global Learning, September 1997.

3. Author interview with Paul Nichols, Director of Training at Arrow Schwebber, Inc., August 1997.

4. R. S. Kaplan and D. P. Norton, *The Balanced Scorecard* (Boston: Harvard Business School Press, 1996), 126–143.

5. Author interview with Patricia Asp, Vice President of ServiceMaster, February 1998.

6. Author interview with Jinny Goldstein, CEO of PBS's The Business Channel, March 1999.

7. M. J. Wheatley, *Leadership and the New Science* (San Francisco: Berrett Koehler, 1994), 75–79.

8. Author interview with Patrick Hernandez, Vice President of Human Resources, New Century Energies, February 1998.

9. Author interview with Sam Reese, Vice President of Kinko's, October 1997.

Chapter 7

1. Buckman Laboratories' sales team at the Knowledge Management Summit, Denver, Colorado, June 1996.

2. Bob Galvin, then Chairman of Motorola, speaking to the US West executive team, October 1995.

3. Don Tapscot, *Growing Up Digital* (New York: McGraw-Hill, 1998), 3, 75–77.

4. W. H. Davidow and M. S. Malone, *The Virtual Corporation* (New York: HarperBusiness, 1992), 184–193.

5. In 1991 the National Association of Manufacturers (NAM), working with consultant Towers Perrin, surveyed 4,000 NAM members about the quality of their workers' job skills. The results were published in a 1992 report.

6. Quote from a memorandum sent to the US West leadership team by Jerry Johnson, June 1995.

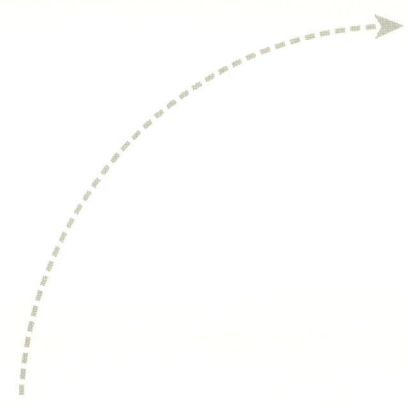

Index

A

Accumulation of experience, 28–29, 71, 72–73

  accelerating, 35–36

  focusing on, 84

  left to chance, 73–77

  managing, 77–78, 76f.

Airframe industry, 90

Alfred P. Sloan museum, 36

American Home Shield, 128

American Society for Training and Development, 89–90

Anderson, John R., 69

Arrow Electronics, 105, 106–107

Asp, Patricia, 111

Assimilation, 28, 71, 75

Automotive industry, 36–37

B

The Balanced Scorecard, 50, 109

Best practice, 105

Boeing Company, 131

Bouchard, Tom, 106

Breakaway. *See also* Rhythm of proficiency

  conditions of, 9

  defined, 7–8

  and proficiency threshold, 61

Brunetti, Wayne, 15

Buckman, Bob, 129–130

Buckman Laboratories, 129–130

Business-to-business companies, and speed, 11–12

C

Cambridge Technology Partners, 136

Candor, 115, 119t.

Cantu, Carlos, 128–129

ChemLawn, 128

Colorado Public Utilities Commission, 20

Competition, 42–43

Condit, Phil, 131

Connectivity, 114

The Customer Comes Second, 135

Customer defection, 21

Customer service

  and training, 20–21

  US West example, 19–21

D

Dell, Michael, 37

Deming, W. Edwards, 56

Dewey, John, 66–67

E

Employee retention, 121–124

Experience, accumulation of. *See* Accumulation of experience

Expertise. *See also* Performance, Proficiency

  faster development of, 12

  as key element of company's brand, 13

  and marketing, 15

Breakaway

Breakaway

Translation, 28, 71–72, 75
TruGreen, 128

U

United Parcel Service, 93
U.S. Department of Labor, 123
US West, 19–20, 93, 130

V

Value chain, 21
    internal, 56–61, 59f., 60t.
    links, 53–56, 53f.
    and proficiency threshold, 54t.,
      60t.
Value proposition, 21
    attributes, 50–52, 51f., 57
    image, 50
    internal, 59f.
    product and service, 50
    and promises, 42
    and rapid delivery, 29–31
    relationships, 50